FAMILY GROWTH

ELECTIVES

Parenting Streetwise Kids

Studies for Parents of Kids at Risk

Victoria Johnson and Mike Murphy

David C. Cook Publishing Co., Elgin, Illinois—Paris, Ontario

850 N. Grove Ave., Elgin, IL 60120-2892
Cable address: DCCOOK
Cover designers: Tom Schild and Jack Foster
Cover illustrator: Pete Whyte
Illustrator: Guy Wolek
Product Developer: Terri Hibbard
Edited by Dave and Neta Jackson
Printed in U.S.A.

ISBN: 0-7814-5137-X

1 2 3 4 5 6 7 8 9 10

Contents

Welcome to Family Growth Electives

Congratulations! The fact that you are using a study in the Family Growth Electives series says that you are concerned about today's families. You and your group of parents are about to begin an exciting adventure.

Each course in this series has been created with today's families in mind. Rather than taking a single topic and applying it to all adults, these Family Growth Electives treat each adult life stage or situation separately. This means that people who are approaching or going through similar stages in life can get together to share and study their common needs from a biblical perspective.

The concept of family life stages comes from the work of Dr. Dennis B. Guernsey, associate professor of Marital and Family Therapy, Fuller Theological Seminary. Guernsey says that the family has critical tasks to accomplish at each stage in order to nurture healthy Christians.

Many adults in churches today have not come from strong Christian roots. Others may have attended church as children, drifted away during their adolescent or young adult years, and are now back in church in an effort to get help with the everyday problems of family life.

Some adults do not have the benefits of living near their extended family. The church can meet the needs of such people by becoming their "family." It can also help strengthen families by teaching them biblical principles and giving opportunities for applying those principles. That's exactly what you'll be doing as you lead your group in this Family Growth Electives study.

Dave and Neta Jackson, Editors

Introduction

This course is for parents who know that their neighborhood is too violent for the welfare of the children who are growing up in it. There's crack on the streets and guns in the schools, and even your own front step isn't a safe place to pass an afternoon.

The *U.S. News and World Report* recently estimated that more than three million crimes a year are committed in or near the eighty-five thousand U.S. public schools. A University of Michigan study reported that 9 percent of eighth graders carry a gun, knife, or club to school at least once a month. In all, an estimated 270,000 guns go to school every day. Twenty percent of suburban high schoolers surveyed by Tulane University researchers thought it was appropriate to shoot someone "who has stolen something from you." Eight percent believed it is all right to shoot a person who had "done something to offend or insult you."[1]

A generation ago, white families used to flee to the suburbs to escape what frightened them about the city. Many ethnic families do not have that option. But even if it were available, it would be small comfort. Today, while you can run, you cannot hide! While big cities may still have the greatest number of kids involved in gangs, the largest growth of gang activity today is occurring in small towns and rural areas.

So how can the children of the parents in your group survive and even thrive in our violent society?

In this course, your group members will gain a biblical perspective and learn many helpful tips about how families can cope with the violence in the society around them as they participate in the active learning in this course. You'll find activities for group members to do alone, as couples, in small groups, and with the entire group together.

As the leader, you will find this course easy to prepare and easy to use. You do not have to be an expert yourself. Each forty-five- to sixty-minute session includes step-by-step instructions printed in regular type. Each session begins with "Getting Ready" which lists everything you need to do before group time. To help you pace yourself according to your available time, there are suggested time frames for each step.

All content is Scripture-based. At the beginning of each session plan you will find a list of the Scriptures to be covered.

Things you might say aloud to your group are in **bold type**. Of course, it is always best to restate things in your own words. Suggested answers to questions are in parentheses.

Each of the thirteen sessions has reproducible Resource sheets. In most cases you will use these as handouts for group members. It would also work to turn some Resources into overhead transparencies if you'd like.

Parenting Streetwise Kids can be a source of encouragement and growth for your group members. By using this Family Growth Elective, you will nurture growth in the lives of your adults—growth in their relationship with the Lord, each other, and their children.

1. Thomas Toch, "Violence in the Schools," *U.S. News and World Report*, November 8, 1993, pp. 31-35, as reported in Focus on the Family newsletter, January 1994, 5.

Looking Back

1

Session Aim:

Session Aim:
To have parents examine their own "growing up" and the role violence played then compared to now; to identify sin as the root cause of violence.

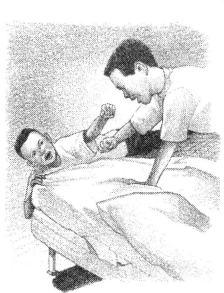

*I*n his book *Childhood*, Bill Cosby, tells about nighttime fights with his younger brother Russell. They shared the same bed, and Bill would start things rolling with, "Don't touch my side of the bed, Russell. This is my side, and I don't want you on it."

Russell would respond, "What do you mean, 'Your side of the bed?' Ain't nobody owns a side."

"Well, I do," Bill would argue, "and I don't want your body touching my side."

At this point Russell would get tough, "I'll touch any side of this bed I want."

A few comments more and the bed became a boxing ring. Then Dad would call, "Quiet down or I'm bringin' my belt."

Bill would turn to his brother and say, "If you don't shut up, Dad's comin' in with his belt and it'll rip the meat off your bones. You'll wish I was hittin' you again."

"Well, you hit me in the eye," Russell would whimper. And round two commenced.

Can you remember similar childhood fights? Can you recall the excitement of a good five-minute playground brawl, before the principal or teacher broke it up? For some, these aren't the only kind of violent childhood memories.

Sometimes we want to pretend that violence is something new. That is part of having a selective memory. We need to admit what *was* so that we can deal effectively with what *is* in this more violent society in which we find ourselves.

*I*t is important for the participants to acknowledge that violence was present when they were young. . . .

Getting Ready

Scriptures:
Genesis 4:1-13; Galatians 5:19-21; James 4:1-7.

1. Make one photocopy of "Memories" (RS-1A), and cut up the sheet into individual "memories." Place these into a hat for distribution to the group members.
2. Photocopy enough copies of "Violence: Yesterday and Today" (RS-1B) for everyone in the group.
3. Photocopy more than enough copies of "Kids Speak Out" (RS-1C) for every parent so that those parents who are interested in surveying more than one child can do so.
4. Be sure to have extra paper for those who might need it.

❶ When I Was Young

Objective:
To give parents an opportunity to get to know each other and to reflect on their growing up years (15 minutes).

As a warm-up have everyone introduce themselves, share the ages of their children, and briefly state why they decided to attend this group. Pass the hat with "Memories." Have everyone take a slip of paper and respond based on their experiences as a child or adolescent.

For this exercise it is more fun if people can try to remember what was happening when they were in either junior high or senior high. If someone feels uncomfortable with the "memory" he or she has drawn, allow that person to pick a new one. Have fun with this. It is okay if people "hitchhike" off of what someone else says and describes, for instance, their own memory of their favorite hangout even though that slip was drawn by someone else.

After everyone shares, ask the participants what they see as the biggest difference between growing up in today's world as compared to the world they grew up in. Jot down general observations on the board.

❷ Violence: Yesterday and Today

Objective:
To have group members explore their perceptions of the levels of violence present today as compared to when they were growing up (15 minutes).

Focus the discussion on the issue of violence by distributing copies of "Violence: Yesterday and Today" (RS-1B). Have participants spend a few moments filling out the work sheet. Have them jot notes in each box that will help them remember their impressions for the subsequent discussion. Details are not important.

You might need to help people reflect on the nature of violence when they were growing up. For instance, you can prime the pump by reading the remarks in the introduction or by introducing your own thoughts. It is important for the participants to acknowledge that violence was present when they were young, though they may have felt very sheltered from its reality.

Do not be afraid to give them hints. For instance, the nightly news brought us the violence of the Civil Rights Movement, the Vietnam War, the '68 National Democratic Convention, the assassination of national leaders, and widespread rioting.

It is possible people won't remember some things. That's okay. Our culture was at a different place years ago. The theme of violence didn't capture people's attention and fears the way it does today.

Explore ways they think our society has changed: **What have been some of the big changes that have occurred since we were kids? How have these changes impacted our culture? Have these contributed in any way to the development of a more violent society?** Allow a few moments for response. Do not try to get parents to offer specific answers. Even no answer is okay. This is only to get them thinking.

Educator Jawanza Kunjufu says 1963 was a significant year. It was the year prayer was taken out of schools. In his book *Hip-Hop vs. MAAT,* **he reports the negative effects of this decision. After the removal of prayer, the Bible, the Ten Commandments, many traditional moral values, etc. were also rejected. Sexually transmitted diseases, premarital sex, pregnancies, abortions, divorce rates, and the number of violent crimes all significantly increased after the removal of prayer in schools.**[1]

Gordon McLean, in *Cities of Lonesome Fear: God Among the Gangs,* **identifies four major changes which have affected our children.** List and number the underlined phrases on the board as you come to them.

When kids seem to be spinning out of control, some parents try to regain their footing by recalling, "Back when I was your age . . ." But few, if any, contemporary adults ever lived in an age such as this. Not many of us grew up going to school where violence was a fact of daily life and coke (the illegal drug) was easier to get than a Coke [the carbonated drink].

The enormous changes that have created this

different world did not happen overnight. By talking with parents about how it was when they were young, we see patterns of change emerging.

- First, kids lost their innocence when television became a staple in the home, presenting lifestyles that are alien and offensive to traditional families as normal and acceptable.
- Then kids lost their respect for social mores (beliefs, customs, traditions, manners) as the drug culture offered the challenge to "tune in, turn on, and drop out."
- Next, kids lost their values as intellectuals proclaimed, "God is dead," and everything sacred was up for grabs.
- Finally, kids have lost their hope. This is the first generation that does not see itself living better than its parents, a sure sign of the impact of worldwide economic and social upheaval. "So why get an education?" many young people ask. "Nobody's going anywhere." The key words for many urban kids in the nineties are alone, fear, despair.[2]

Generate discussion with these comments and questions:

Name some negative behaviors that are often portrayed on television as normal and acceptable. (Premarital sex, defiant talk to parents, drinking at teen parties, and disrespect for authority.)

In what ways did the drug culture challenge traditional mores? (Insobriety is cool. Hard work is foolish. The "establishment" is something to scorn, not join and improve.)

What attitudes result when society abandons its common belief in God? (Common standards of right and wrong disappear. Purpose in living is eroded. Motivation to serve others is diminished.)

How have modern kids lost hope? (If life is meaningless, there is no reason to try and do better in any area.)

❸ The Root of Violence

Objective:
To identify sin as the root cause of violence (10 minutes).

Have the people open their Bibles. Ask for volunteers to read the following Scriptures. After each one, encourage discussion on the source of violence by asking the suggested questions.

Genesis 4:1-13

What was the source of Cain's hatred of his brother? (He was jealous and angry that God did not look with favor on his offering like He did on Abel's sacrifice. Some respondents may suggest that Cain disobeyed God by trying to bring a vegetable offering when God desired a blood sacrifice. God had provided that example by preparing skin clothes to cover the nakedness of Adam and Eve's sin [see Gen. 3:21], but there is no record that God had previously made that a requirement for an acceptable sacrifice. At the very least, Cain refused to be corrected.)

What are the implications for society if people accept or adopt Cain's attitude, "Am I my brother's keeper"? (It is always God's intention that we live in community, caring for one another. The attitude that we don't need to do this, breeds and encourages violence.)

Galatians 5:19-21

What are the consequences for those who persist in or defend sinful behaviors? (They "will not inherit the kingdom of God.")

James 4:1-7

The King James Version asks, "From whence come wars and fightings among you?" How would you answer this question? (The passage identifies sin as the source, but let the group personalize this in regard to the violence about which they are concerned.)

The authors of *Gangs in America* write, "Blacks killing Blacks is the number one cause of death among African-American youth in the United States."[3] In light of this statement, how would you answer the question in James: "From whence come wars and fightings among you?" (This question is to stimulate discussion, not to solicit a specific answer.)

Summarize the Bible study by making this point: **Violence is a symptom of a spiritual problem. It is a direct consequence of sin. It may result because of greed, envy, dispair, or other sinful motivations.** Discuss: **How is this ancient record—the Bible—relevant to our world today?** If you have nonbelievers in your group, this may be a good opportunity to identify and discuss the Bible as God's reliable Word to us.

❹ Listen to What Kids Say about Violence

Objective:

To encourage parents to discuss with their children common forms of violence present in their schools and neighborhoods and to have parents state one way they hope this course will help them (5-20 minutes).

Distribute copies of "Kids Speak Out" (RS-1C), encouraging those who wish to survey more than one child to take extra copies. Urge the participants to explore the topic of violence with their own children by using the questionnaire. Older children can fill out the form on their own. Parents can administer the questionnaire to younger children.

Explain that this questionnaire can be very useful in helping parents dialog with their children. Dialog is a skill that needs to be in every parent's toolbox of effective parenting. Caution the parents that this should not be a time for scolding or arguing with their children. They are trying to explore their kids' perceptions about violence.

Tell the parents that they should bring the completed questionnaire back to the next session of the group. Not only are we trying to get information from the children in this exercise but we are trying to provide a way of talking about a very important issue. So, encourage parents to follow-through with this exercise.

Once you have passed out the questionnaire, share the following information compiled from *Youth Worker Update* to give the parents some perspective.

- One in five females has been a victim of sexual assault, in most cases by someone she knew. In a third of the cases, the assailant was another student.
- One in three teens knows someone who has brought a weapon to school.
- Forty-two percent of the males have access to one or more firearms.
- More than half reported frequent fights between students.
- Five percent said there had been a shooting on school grounds, and 7 percent reported a knife fight.

- Seventeen percent reported that a teacher in their school had been assaulted.
- One third considered suicide.[4]

To close this session, have the parents use the back of either RS-1A or RS-1B to complete this statement. **"I hope this course will help me. . . ."** Encourage the group members to keep this statement for evaluation at the end of the course.

In you have a full hour for group time, invite the parents to share their statements with the whole group and report on their own experience or concerns about violence. Begin by asking for volunteers, rather than going around the circle as sharing may be an emotional thing for some. Maybe their child has been involved in violence or threatened at school or in the neighborhood. Maybe drug activity is going on in their neighborhood. Some may even have "lost" a child to a gang, prison, or even death. If the group is developing a warm and safe environment, you might invite "holdouts" to share near the end, but don't pressure people.

Close by praying for several of the needs expressed in the sharing time. If you did not have time for the final sharing, pray for the group's experience and the general needs of our children.

Remind parents to bring their completed surveys for next session.

Notes:

1. Jawanza Kunjufu, *Hip-Hop vs. MAAT* (Chicago: African American Images, 1993), 99-106.
2. Gordon McLean with Dave and Neta Jackson, *Cities of Lonesome Fear: God Among the Gangs* (Chicago: Moody Press, 1991), 66, 67. Underlining added.
3. Wendell Amstutz and Bart Larson, *Gangs in America* (Rochester, Minn.: National Counseling Resource Center, 1993), 55.
4. Compiled from *Youth Worker Update, Newsletter for Christian Youth Workers*, December 1993, 5.

Bang, Bang You're Dead

2

Session Aim:
To examine the impact of violence on children and adults.

Please help me! Last week, Allen, my fifteen-year-old nephew got into an argument with a seventeen-year-old neighborhood boy. The older boy cursed at my nephew and pushed him around. The boys who watched told the story like this.

"After Greg pushed Allen, Allen stood there for a minute, as though he was going to fight back. Then Allen just took off running. We thought he was just mad and went home to blow off some steam. We went on playing ball. About ten minutes later, Allen came back, pulled out a pistol and shot Greg. Popped him, just like that!"

Before this tragedy, Allen seemed okay, just a typical teenager. At the last family gathering he laughed along with us as we reminisced about our crazy teenage years. Sure, my sister occasionally had to talk to Allen's teachers when he fell behind in his school work, and he had gotten into a fist fight or two. But those seemed like ordinary, growing up problems. We never imagined he would do something like this.

As I write this, I can hear my own two boys in the next room arguing over whose turn it is as they play Nintendo. I'm concerned about them. Is there something specific I should watch for? How can I prevent this tragedy from happening to them? I'm afraid, very afraid!

—*A worried mother*

When secular analysts look at problems, they tend to focus on the symptoms, rather than the causes.

Getting Ready
Scriptures:
Romans 1:18-32; II Timothy 3:1-5; Mark 9:33-37; 10:13-16.

1. Make photocopies of "Survey Result Questions" (RS-2A), "Listen to the Children" (RS-2B), and "Parents Look at Violence" (RS-2C), for everyone in the class.
2. For the "Violence Continuum" in Step 1 make two signs: "Violence: No Impact (1)" and "Violence: Big Impact (10)." Arrange the room according to the instructions in Step 1.
3. Bring newspaper clippings of violent incidents from your local newspaper.
4. Optional: a tape player and cassette with soft instrumental music for use in Step 3.
5. Be sure you have completed the survey from last week, "Kids Speak Out" (RS-1C) with several kids so you can share results in Step 3 of this session.

❶ Hitting Us Where It Hurts

Objective:
To focus attention on the reality of violence in our midst (10-15 minutes).

Begin the session by having the group create a living "Violence Continuum" as explained below:

Clear a large space in your room. At one end place a chair with a sign on it reading, "Violence: No Impact (1)." At the other end of the space, place a chair with a sign on it reading, "Violence: Big Impact (10)." Explain to the group that as you announce various things that violence impacts, they should arrange themselves between the two signs as though they were standing on a continuum where their position represents their opinion from "1" (no impact) to "10" (big impact).

After you read each statement and the parents have taken their positions, have them take turns sharing why they are standing where they are. If your group is large, you may want them to share only with the person nearest them so that the sharing will not take so long.

a. Impact of violence on our culture
b. Impact of violence on your kids
c. Impact of violence on you personally
d. Impact of violence on your neighborhood

Have the parents help you rearrange the chairs and take their seats. Then read the account by "a worried mother" on page 14. Stimulate a brief discussion by asking: **What recent examples of violence in our community can you recall?** Have local newspaper clippings ready as examples if the group does not quickly respond. List all examples on the board.

This generation is in need of a resurrection and the new life Jesus Christ offers.

❷ Dealing with Causes Rather Than Symptoms

Objective:
To reinforce the concept of "sin" as the root cause of violence (15 minutes).

In Session 1 the root cause of evil and violence was identified as sin. (Scriptures from Session 1: Genesis 4:1-13—jealousy, anger and the lack of caring motivated Cain to murder Abel. Galatians 5:19-21—the hatred, discord, jealousy, and rage that come from the sinful nature cannot be part of the kingdom of God. James 4:1-7—the source of conflict is selfishness.) But this root cause is not acknowledged by many secular analysts.

Ask the group to discuss, **What do you think secular analysts such as many counselors, teachers, or politicians point to as the problem for violence in our society?** Allow the group to freely offer their opinions, then read a quote from *Cities of Lonesome Fear: God Among the Gangs* by Gordon McLean, the director of the juvenile justice ministry of Metro Chicago Youth for Christ.

> **When secular analysts look at problems, they tend to focus on the symptoms, rather than causes. Listen to the observations of a group of counselors.**
> • **"The home, school, and church used to act as a restraint on youthful behavior."**
> • **"There is usually just a mother alone raising a family."**
> • **"Some parents use alcohol themselves."**
> • **"Parents attack each other."**
> • **"There is no one for kids to talk to."**[1]

These statements describe what many consider are the causes of a generation gone wild. But, from a Christian perspective, they describe symptoms of a spiritually dead generation. This generation is in need of a resurrection and the new life Jesus Christ offers.

Ask: **What are some of the solutions commonly given for the violence problem?** (Stabilize the school system, more money for community programs, eliminate racism, more jobs, better law enforcement system, death penalty, etc.)

It is true, educational inequalities, lack of family stability, employment issues, racism, etc., contribute to the development of a violent culture. Christians need to be involved, helping to resolve these important issues. God cares deeply about anyone feeling the "sting of sin," and so should we.

However, a trap we need to avoid is assuming that

exploitation, violence, racism, etc. will disappear if and when secular solutions are implemented. The problem is deeper than surface resolutions. It's a sinful heart problem. Sin creates trouble. When the spiritual dimension is neglected, we start to believe in human abilities and to solve problems by leaning on self, not God. Too often spiritual strategies become secondary, instead of primary resources.

Break the class into two groups. Assign one group to study Romans 1:18-32 and the other group to study II Timothy 3:1-5. Have them identify the sins mentioned in their respective passages, noting in which verse(s) the sin is mentioned. Have one person in each group record the findings.

While the groups are working on the Scripture passages, prepare the chalkboard or marker board with two headings: on the left, "Violent Activities," and on the right, "Sins Identified in Scripture." Spaced several "lines" apart under the left heading list these acts: Rapes, Muggings, Murders, Beatings.

When you reconvene the group, ask the teams to report on the sins they found in the passages. When a sin is listed, ask the group: **To which violent act might that sin lead?** Record their responses accordingly on the board. It may look like this with the italicized entries being the group's contributions:

Violent Activities	Sinful Attitudes or Actions Identified in Scripture
Rapes	Romans 1:18, 24—*Godlessness, impurity*
	II Timothy 3:2, 3—*Abusive, without self-control, brutal, unholy*
Muggings	Romans 1:25, 29—*Serve the creature rather than the Creator, greed*
	II Timothy 3:3, 4—*Lovers of self and money*
Murders	Romans 1:28—*Depraved minds*
	II Timothy 3:2—*Loveless, treacherous*
Beatings	Romans 1:31—*Heartless, ruthless*
	II Timothy 3:3, 4—*Brutal and rash*

Too often we look at the symptoms of sin as the issue, rather than sin itself.

Have someone read Romans 1:24, 25. **According to these verses, why do people get involved in violent activities ?** ("God gave them over in the sinful desires of their hearts." God allowed their sinful appetites to take control. "They exchanged the truth of God for a lie, and worshiped and served created things rather than the Creator." People are naturally more interested in things, rather than God.)

In what ways is sin like a cancer? (Both claim victims. Sometimes the victims are obvious: a person is shot, a woman raped, a child abused, or a leg is lost, surgery is required, strength is lost. Both can also spread—initially, at least—without any indication. Potential victims see their freedom limited because of fear, it affects the mind, generates doubt, raises barriers between people, etc. Both start small and continue to grow until they affect a wide area, incapacitating the victims.)

Why is it important to identify sin as the root cause of violence? (If a person with cancer only tries to treat the pain, he or she will not be cured. We want to treat the true disease, not merely the symptoms. As Christians, we must always look at the spiritual dimension of any problem we face. That is our starting point in discussing the issues. Too often we look at the symptoms of sin as the issue, rather than sin itself.)

❸ What Do Kids Say about Violence?

Objective:
To discuss the response of children toward violence (10-15 minutes).

Pass out "Survey Result Questions" (RS-2A) and "Listen to the Children" (RS-2B). Break the participants into groups of three or four to work on the sheets. Make sure at least one person in the group has a completed survey. Have them follow the instructions on both work sheets. If you completed surveys with kids, you could share your results at this point. If no one in the group was able to complete the survey, move on to "Listen to the Children."

Bring the group back together and read Mark 9:33-37 and 10:13-16. (Option: If you have a cassette, play soft, instrumental music in the background as you read.) Have a time of silent prayer for the young people caught in frightening situations. Then, ask someone to pray out loud about the violence we see, the victims, and the perpetrators.

❹ Evaluating the Impact of Violence on Us Personally

Objective:
To give parents the opportunity to talk about how violence impacts them (10-15 minutes).

Pass out copies of "Parents Look at Violence" (RS-2C). Give the parents a few minutes to fill out the questionnaire, then discuss the questions.

Try to be reassuring and hopeful that the course will attempt to tackle some of these difficult questions and come up with solutions.

Encourage parents to continue talking with their children. Ask the parents to read the work sheet "Listen to the Children" (RS-2B) with their kids. If the children are small, the parents could ask them to draw a picture of their neighborhood. Suggest that they encourage discussion with their children by asking: **What is happening to these children in the article? Why do they feel so frightened? Do you have similar feelings about your neighborhood? Tell me about your picture.**

Close the session by encouraging the parents that in future sessions, more responses and solutions will be suggested. Pray that God will build an atmosphere of openness and trust within the group and that He will give group members His perspective on violence. Ask Him to reveal solutions to problems related to violence and to give a sense of hope to those who are hurting.

Notes:

1. Gordon McLean with Dave and Neta Jackson, *Cities of Lonesome Fear: God Among the Gangs* (Chicago: Moody Press, 1991), 76, 77.

What's On Your Mind?

3

Session Aim:
To identify cultural messages that contribute to a violent climate and explore the impact of those messages on adults.

The National Negro College Fund has coined the phrase, "A mind is a terrible thing to waste." An uneducated mind cripples a person and limits the individual's abilities. However, a spiritually unregenerate mind is under Satan's control and extremely dangerous!

Most parents are very conscientious about getting their children through school. They want their kids to attend college and climb the ladder of success. But are they equally concerned about their Christian education? Do children understand the need for salvation? Are they interested in Jacob's ladder, and getting kids headed for eternal life?

There are several anti-violence campaigns going on in our communities. Politicians launch "Rid our cities of guns" campaigns. Public schools employ metal detectors to keep dangerous weapons out. But we as Christians need to start our own campaign . . . to eliminate un-Christlike attitudes from our minds.

The battle line has been drawn. Satan is daring us to cross over. He has captured numerous young minds. He causes them to do serious damage to themselves and others. God's people have been commanded to reach into Satan's territory and reclaim the lost. And we are also to protect those who have not yet been totally persuaded by his lies.

Could we parents be communicating the very messages we don't want our children receiving?

Getting Ready

Scriptures:
Matthew 19:21-26; 22:37-40; Hebrews 4:12, 13; Romans 3:9-18; 12:2; Exodus 20:1-3; Psalms 8:3-8; 119:1-4; John 15:26; Deuteronomy 26:16-19.

1. On newsprint, an overhead transparency, or the board, create a list of the eleven "-isms" as identified in Step 1. Do not include the cultural messages.
2. Photocopy "Cultural Messages" (RS-3A), and "Violent Acts" (RS-3B), making enough copies for everyone.

❶ The World's Preaching at Us?

Objective:
To examine eleven common cultural messages that permeate our society and influence young and old alike (15 minutes).

Explain: **In this session, we will look at the messages our culture is giving us and focus on how they influence us as adults. Next session we will look at how they impact our children. As parents we are concerned about our children and the negative impact the secular culture has on them. But we are affected by the culture as well.**

Parents are the primary religious educators of their children, which is a serious responsibility. Therefore, periodically we need to examine what is happening to us. Could we parents be communicating the very messages we don't want our children receiving?

There is discussion in religious education circles about the message of the faith becoming a curious mishmash of biblical truth, cultural philosophies, and whatever we heard most recently on talk radio or Oprah. We don't want that to become true for us.

Display the list of eleven "-isms" written ahead of time. Go over the "-isms" inviting the group members to define them and to identify the cultural messages of each one. (Use the suggested answers when needed.) Make sure the group basically agrees that these messages are permeating our culture. In many respects the messages flow together.

1. **Materialism:** The most important thing in life is the ownership of possessions.
2. **Existentialism:** Live for the moment; it's all that you have.
3. **Individualism:** The most important person in your life is you.
4. **Hedonism:** Pleasure, happiness, and fun are the primary purposes of life.
5. **Secularism:** God is not significant. At best He is irrelevant.

6. **Naturalism:** Human life has no more value than an owl or a tree.
7. **Utopianism:** Humans are basically good. Just give them a good environment, and all evil will vanish.
8. **Anti-historicism:** Truth is relative and not as important as being politically correct.
9. **Pragmatism:** If it works do it.
10. **Moral relativism:** No absolutes. There are no rights, no wrongs.
11. **Victimism:** I am the way I am because of what other people have done to me.

Give every group member a copy of "Cultural Messages" (RS-3A), and allow the parents about five minutes to complete columns two and three individually. They will work on scriptural responses (column four) in the next step. Have them break into groups of five or less and discuss their responses in columns 2 ("How is it [the message] being spread?") and column 3 ("How am I affected?"). Be ready to assist if needed according to the following.

How Is It Being Spread?	Spiritual Responses
1. Media, peer pressure, athletic celebrities, advertising	May fulfill wants rather than needs, get-rich schemes
2. Literature, entertainment	Delay decisions with eternal significance
3. Schools, media entertainment	Selfishness, take instead of give, prejudice
4. Arts, media, schools non-Christians	Pursuit of fun, lack of work ethic, entitlement, thrill-seeking
5. Government, literature, theater, schools	Ignore true God
6. "Rights" movements, schools, media	Abortion, euthanasia, casual regard for human life
7. Cults and "-isms," secular philosophies	No urgency to share the Good News

8. Media, entertainment	Leave the moorings of Scripture, rewrite history
9. Self-help movements, books, magazines, TV talk shows	Situation ethics
10. Secular philosophies and psychologies, media, justice system	Situation ethics, decisions based on emotions, not Scripture
11. Talk shows, justice system, schools, TV, entertainment	Sense of helplessness and hopelessness, avoidance of accountability, lack of responsibility

❷ God's Word Responds

Objective:
To examine the Scripture and to begin the process of helping participants filter cultural messages through God's Word (15-25 minutes).

While the group members are still in their small groups, have them study the biblical passages referenced in the right-hand column of their work sheets, filling in what the Scripture has to say about the cultural messages. We are not trying to "proof-text" here, but rather point to the Scripture for advice and counsel. For some individuals this may be difficult. Some are better tuned to messages of the culture than to the Scripture. Be prepared to help them out with suggestions:

1. *Matthew 19:21-25*—(Following Christ may cost us materially.)
2. *Hebrews 4:12, 13*—(We will have to give an account before God.)
3. *Matthew 22:37-40*—(Love your neighbor.)
4. *Romans 12:2*—(Don't allow the world to mold you.)
5. *Exodus 20:1-3*—(Have no other gods before God.)
6. *Psalm 8:3-8*—(We are valuable to God.)
7. *Romans 3:9-18*—(No one is perfectly good, we are all sinners.)
8. *John 15:26*—(The Holy Spirit will help us discern truth.)
9. *Psalm 119:1-4*—(Do things God's way.)
10. *Deuteronomy 26:16-19*—(Obey God's instructions.)
11. *Matthew 19:26*—(With God all things are possible.)

❸ Justifying Violent Acts

Objective:
To see how violent acts can be justified by using cultural messages as the basis for immoral activities (10 minutes).

Pass out copies of "Violent Acts" (RS-3B) and have people pair up with someone other than their spouses. Assign each set of partners four or five "Violent Acts" statements to discuss, asking the question, **"How might the person(s) involved justify their actions based on the cultural messages?"** Some people might disagree about whether or not some of the acts are necessarily violent. That's okay.

❹ How Can We Make Personal Changes?

Objective:
To suggest ways to change negative thinking and behaviors the group has discovered in this session in themselves and their families (5-10 minutes).

Up to this point, we have discussed the messages our culture is trying to make us listen to and obey and how they go against the counsel of God's Word. Let's brainstorm ways we can resist negative forces, individually and within our families. Make two columns on the board and list suggestions. Here are some ideas:

[Column 1] INDIVIDUALLY	[Column 2] FAMILY
Spend more time reading the Bible.	Implement family devotions.
Become aware of what your kids are looking at on TV and listen to some of their music. When you see philosophies being glorified that are not good, say so and explain why.	Spend more time talking to your kids about these influences and why they are not good. Give your children the opportunity to share their perspectives on these issues.
Be committed to make changes in your life when you see yourself following worldly philosophies or acting inconsistently.	Spend time doing activities with another family that is also trying to uphold similar principles.

Before closing in prayer, ask each individual to make a commitment to put at least one suggestion into practice this week in his or her personal life or in the family. Pray for the group and for their commitments.

Battling for Our Youth

4

Session Aim:
To explore the impact of cultural messages on children and begin thinking about ways to counteract them.

Have you ever met people who allow the culture to define who they are and what they do? They work hard at "keeping up with the Joneses." They always have the latest fashion in furniture, hair styles, or clothes. When I watch people like this, I'm amused.

However, if a violent dimension is added to these characteristics, tragedy can be the result.

I remember interacting with a family who bought into every negative cultural message imaginable. One of the sons, Del, went to summer camp with me. We arrived back in town at nine o'clock in the evening. I was awakened by Del's mother around four o'clock the next morning. "Please come with me to the police station. They've arrested Del for murder. He didn't do it. He was at camp with you." As we drove to the police station Del's mother explained to me what happened. What she told me sent chills up my spine. "I'm glad Del was with you. I know he couldn't be involved. But, if he hadn't been with you, he might be the killer. He's like that, you know." Their whole family was living without a moral compass. Del had seemed like a nice kid at camp, but he was in a battle, and his heart, soul, and mind were severely wounded. The culture was winning. His own mother admitted it.

However, there is hope, for Del and others like him.

—Mike Murphy

It is important to note that not everything the culture says is evil.

Getting Ready

Scriptures:
Ephesians 6:10-18;
I John 2:15-17.

1. Make copies of "What Our Kids Are Saying Today" (RS-4A) and "The Whole Armor of God" (RS-4B) for everyone in the group.
2. Make copies of "Kids and the Media" (RS-4C) to be handed out as preparation for Session 5. Make extra copies to have on hand next session for those who might forget to bring their copies to group. This resource includes four pages.

❶ Cultural Messages Bombarding Our Kids

Objective:
To examine the cultural messages that are being communicated to our children (10 minutes).

Last week we examined the impact of cultural messages on parents. In this session we want to look at the same messages again, but this time in terms of how they affect our children.

It is important to note that not everything the culture says is evil. We want to avoid extreme culture bashing or developing an "us" versus "them" attitude.

We are affected positively and negatively by our culture. We can enjoy great works of art, stirring music, and a variety of sports. We should be challenged as Christians when we discover secular institutions or persons expressing more compassion for the poor than do our churches or ourselves. It is important to acknowledge non-Christian performers and artists who have touched us in profound ways. God, of course, is the author of all that is beautiful. His hand is always at work, and we reap the benefit.

We will not explore all cultural aspects in depth nor give a balanced perspective on the whole culture. Our objective is to explain how cultural pressures or "-isms" —as we called them last time—contribute to an environment in which violence thrives.

Have the participants work independently on "What Our Kids Are Saying Today" (RS-4A). When they have finished, go over the comments, identifying the "-ism" represented by each one.

1. "If my old man was rich, then I could make it." (k. Victimism.)

2. "Yeah, I cheated. So what? I passed the test didn't I?" (i. Pragmatism.)

3. "I blew it this time, but give me time. I'll get better." (g. Utopian.)

4. "What's God ever done for me?" (e. Secularism.)

5. "Everybody else has the latest video recorder and we've got this old one." (a. Materialism.)

6. "What about me?" (c. Individualism.)

7. "When you die, that's it, right?" (f. Naturalism.)

8. "Just because it's wrong for you, doesn't mean it's wrong for me." (j. Moral relativism.)

9. "I'm going to enjoy myself as much as possible, now. Tomorrow may never come." (b. Existentialism.)

10. "Party hearty!" Have a good time. (d. Hedonism.)

11. "All politicians lie, so what?" (h. Anti-historicism.)

After going over the matching exercise, invite parents to share comments their own children might say. Then ask, **Is your son or daughter buying into these kind of messages? How could these messages be a building block toward violence in the lives of young people?** (Not every "-ism" has an obvious violent product, but here are some. *Materialism:* hurting someone for something you want. *Individualism, hedonism, and secularism:* Combine to suggest that we do what gives us a thrill even if someone gets hurt. *Naturalism:* Abortion or euthanasia. *Pragmatism:* Doing whatever it takes [even murder or abuse] to get what you want. *Victimism:* Child or spouse abuse as modeled by parents. *Moral Relativism:* Do whatever you want, even take another person's life, if necessary.)

❷ The Nature of the Battle

Objective:
To establish the spiritual dimension of the battle for our children's minds and hearts (10 minutes).

According to author Fran Sciacca, "There is a battle for the hearts and minds of teenagers today."[1] Some parents feel that they're in a losing battle. To win, they need to see the seriousness of the situation and to seek God's solutions.

The following statistics have been compiled to demonstrate the impact of Satan's attack against African-American and other children:

We are in a spiritual battle with God on one side and Satan on the other.

- Homicide is the leading cause of death for black males and females.[2]
- Some observers reported that 80 percent of the looters in the South Central L.A. riots after the Rodney King verdict were Hispanic.[3]
- Blacks account for 44 percent of all homicide victims, even though they make up only 12 percent of the population.[4]
- Ninety-five percent of black homicides were committed by black perpetrators.[5]
- There were 728 liquor stores in South Los Angeles before the riots following the Rodney King verdict—more than two and a half times as many as in the state of Rhode Island with twice the population.[6]
- Immigration and Naturalization Service officials estimate that as many as seven thousand women are smuggled into the United States by Asian gangs to become prostitutes in gang-run houses in New York and San Francisco.[7]
- In the ten largest urban cities, the high school dropout rate for black males is 72 percent.[8]
- Nearly 80 percent of black youth live in poverty.[9]
- Unemployment among black youth between the ages of sixteen and nineteen is around 32 percent nationwide.[10]
- In 1960, 78 percent of black families with children were headed by both a mother and a father—a figure which dropped to 37 percent by 1990.[11]
- At the end of the '80s, more than half of African-American children were born to single mothers.[12]
- African-American men and women are finding it difficult to handle responsibilities and turning to alcohol and drugs.[13]

These seem like devastating statistics. But we can win this battle, and the Word of God tells us how.

Have everyone turn to Ephesians 6:10-18. Have volunteers read a verse or two.

What kind of battle is described here, and who are the opposing forces? (We are in a spiritual battle with God on one side and Satan on the other.)

What is necessary for victory in this kind of battle? (Dependence on God's strength and the whole armor of God.)

T he "world" is not trees and flowers, but all that stands against God.

Distribute copies of "The Whole Armor of God" (RS-4B) and allow time for each person to answer the questions individually according to the instructions.

If some of the group members are not yet Christians, this is a good time to explain salvation based on faith in Christ's provision for sin. If possible, talk individually with anyone who expresses an interest in becoming a Christian or wants more information about any of the pieces of "armor."

Have extra copies of the work sheet for parents to work through with their children at home. Encourage them to explain the spiritual defenses in terms the children can understand. This will help moms and dads see where their children's "armor" is weak so they will be able to pray more specifically with and for them.

❸ Battle Plans

Objective:
To get group members to think creatively about conveying God's truth to their children (10-15 minutes).

What are some of the creative ways Satan relays his messages? (Movies, music, video, news coverage, talk shows, etc.) **Satan is a master at peddling illicit sex, illegal drugs, and violence. He has made it into a seductive art form, and his message appeals to kids. One way he works is to convince kids that their wants are really needs. How can we combat Satan's tactics and strategies?**

Have everyone turn to I John 2:15-17 while a volunteer reads the verses.

This persuasive passage gives the key to the Christian's battle strategy. It encourages us to position ourselves on the high, strategic ground, where we will have the advantage over Satan. What is that strategic ground and how is it different from vulnerable ground? (The strategic ground has to do with goals, motives, and obedience to God's commands. When we crave the things of the world, we immediately become vulnerable to Satan's suggestions for how to acquire them and those methods often involve sin.) Note that the "world" is not trees and flowers, but all that stands against God.

This passage also includes a promise for those who do the will of God. This can be a scriptural reference point as we try to help our kids deal with cultural messages. It is an encouraging portion of God's Word to meditate on and to share with our children. Where is

our allegiance? To God or to the world? How is this allegiance evident in our daily lives?

Divide the group into four teams. Assign each team one of the sentences in I John 2:15-17.

Group 1: "Do not love the world or anything in the world."

Group 2: "If anyone loves the world, the love of the Father is not in him."

Group 3: "For everything in the world—the cravings of sinful man, the lust of his eyes and the boasting of what he has and does—comes not from the Father but from the world."

Group 4: "The world and its desires pass away, but the man who does the will of God lives forever."

Instruct the teams to rewrite their assigned section of the passage so it would make sense to a youth. Remind the teams to keep in mind the present battle for the hearts and minds of our kids. When the teams have completed their "modern translation," reconvene the group, and put together the rewritten verses and read them. Here are possible answers:

"Do not love the world or anything in the world."—(Don't depend on the things this world offers for your happiness.)

"If anyone loves the world, the love of the Father is not in him."—(When you spend all of your time and effort trying to get ahead, acquire things, or make a name for yourself, it shows that you really do not love God.)

"For everything in the world—the cravings of sinful man, the lust of his eyes and the boasting of what he has and does—comes not from the Father but from the world." —(Desiring things that God says no to [like sex outside of marriage], wanting to buy everything you see, and thinking too highly of yourself because of money or a job are attitudes which do not come from God.)

"The world and its desires pass away, but the man who does the will of God lives forever."—(Money, recognition, power, all of these things will last a short time, but if you follow God's instructions, you will be most satisfied in this life and in heaven.)

Christians need to learn how to creatively communicate spiritual truth and grab the attention of our youth.

❹ Armed for the Battle

Objective:

To begin the process of counteracting cultural messages being thrust upon our kids (10-15 minutes).

Our kids receive messages of all kinds from many sources, but what kind of messages do we want them to receive? (Follow Jesus. Be responsible. Avoid influence by the wrong crowd. Help the elderly and needy. Love and respect your parents. Work hard for things that last.)

Have you noticed how well the secular culture delivers its messages to people? Commercials are humorous. Movies are filled with action and suspense. Talk shows catch your attention with their "You may think you have heard everything, but listen to this" techniques.

How can parents and the church present truths from God's Word in a way that kids will take notice?

Allow the group to discuss this question. There isn't one correct answer, and it will be important to be respectful of any who question certain contemporary communication techniques. For instance, someone may think that Christian rock or rap music can be employed effectively. Another may think that we don't need to adopt the "world's methods" to communicate God's truth. However, if the group's conversation takes that turn, challenge the group members to offer something else that's better. Encourage them to provide examples of methods that have proved effective in today's culture.

Christians need to learn how to creatively communicate spiritual truth and grab the attention of our youth. This exercise is designed to help the parents communicate and think about creative responses to dangerous messages.

Divide the group into teams of three or four again. Give two sheets of paper to each team. Ask everyone to get out their copy of "What Our Kids Are Saying Today" (RS-4A) that they used in Step 1. Assign each team two or three of the cultural messages—depending on how many teams you have. Ask the teams to create alternative slogans, suitable for wearing on a T-shirt (by their sons or daughters), which counters the secular cultural messages. It should be a slogan a young person would feel comfortable wearing. It shouldn't be embarrassing, sound preachy, adult-like, or boring.

Have the teams share with the whole group the T-shirt slogans they have come up with. Then take a poll, voting on the best one. Have fun with this.

The purpose of this exercise is not to suggest that wearing T-shirts with slogans is the only or the best way to communicate God's truths. Rather, it will encourage group members to think in ways that might communicate to today's kids. Several things can be gained from this exercise. Discuss the difficulty of coming up with something the kids might actually wear.

Ask: **Why was it so hard?** (Maybe we are not used to thinking creatively about how to package God's truth. God's truth is countercultural and slogans against God are easy to come up with.)

The young person today whose life represents the truth of God's Word stands out. To wear a T-shirt that boldly declares a Christian principle would require a commitment and risk ridicule. That is why we need to realize the seriousness of the battle we are in.

Ask: **What characterizes a battle?** (Battles are never easy, and there are casualties. To win the battle, one needs a strategy, and a plan). **Some of the best strategists and planners might be against Christ, but we should not despair. God knows how to plan too. In fact He is the master designer of all things. God is very imaginative. He can give us a variety of ingenious ideas to reach our youth for Christ. Maybe we should ask Him for His ideas.**

❺ The Learning Circle

Objective:
To have group members share about what they learned from today's session (5-10 minutes).

Have people stand in a circle. If you have a large group or are short on time, form two or three smaller circles. Go around each circle asking everyone to complete this sentence: **"An insight I gained today is _____ ."** (For instance, someone might say, "An insight I gained today is that I should not despise any means God uses to reach kids.")

Close in prayer in the same circle.

Preparation for Session 5: Pass out copies of "Kids and the Media" (RS-4C), asking the participants to read through it before the next session and to bring the resource sheet when they return to group the next time. Warn your group members that they may be shocked by some of the facts presented in this material. Point out that the purpose of this resource is to help parents become more aware of what their kids are exposed to.

Close in prayer, asking God to give each parent wisdom as he or she battles for the minds of today's kids.

Notes:

1. Fran Sciacca, *Generation At Risk: What Legacy Are the Baby Boomers Leaving Their Kids?* (Chicago: Moody Press, 1990), 22.

2. Carl C. Bell with Esther J. Jenkins, "Preventing Black Homicide," *The State of Black America 1990* (New York: National Urban League, January 1990), 143-155.

3. Elena Neuman, "Stores of Rage," *Insight on the News*, Sept. 7, 1992, 10ff.

4. Ibid.

5. Ibid.

6. Ibid.

7. Susan Moran, "New World Havens of Oldest Profession," *Insight on the News*, June 21, 1993, 12ff.

8. Marvin McMickel, "Black Men: Endangered Species," *ClubDate*, August/September 1989, 29.

9. U.S. Bureau of Census, 1990.

10. Ibid.

11. Andrew Billingsley, "Understanding African-American Family Diversity," *The State of Black America 1990*, 89-90.

12. Andrew W. Edwards, "The Black Family: A Unique Social System in Transition," *The State of Black Cleveland 1989* (Cleveland: Urban League of Greater Cleveland, 1989), 187.

13. Willie Richardson, *The Black Family* (Grand Rapids, Mich.: Zondervan, 1990), 14.

The Media Made Me Do It!

5

Session Aim:

To help parents examine their children's relationship to the media and its messages and devise a plan for dealing with the negative aspects of the media.

If you were born in the late fifties or early sixties, you probably remember the old "Superfly" movies. The movies influenced black men to wear pastel-colored bell bottom suits, sun glasses, and a coke spoon in the shape of a cross around their necks. Everybody wanted to be Superfly.

The movie *Roots* had its impact in various ways during its week-long showing. A nurse working in the labor and deliver unit of a local hospital said, "I can't believe how many mothers named their babies Kunta Kenta and Kizzy this week." They were main characters in *Roots*.

Recently, how many "Xs" have we seen on caps and T-shirts since Spike Lee's movie *Malcolm X*?

The media motivates our behavior. Unfortunately, the influence is not always positive. One of Satan's prime tools to destroy the lives of people is the media.

Our young people are media-oriented. They hear and see things we never dreamed of when we were young. They get a pretty unhealthy dose of violent images on a daily basis.

What impact does the media have on your child and his or her friends? What can we do to help our children become more discerning in their media intake?

Children who have been extensively influenced by . . . the media might be called "culturally relevant, media-oriented children."

Getting Ready:

Scriptures:
Exodus 20:3, 4, 7, 8, 12-17;
Matthew 4:10; 5:22, 28, 34;
12:36; Luke 12:15; 16:13.

1. You will need three sheets of newsprint or butcher paper and colored markers for each group for use in Step 1.
2. Cut a copy of "Hollywood vs. God's Commandments" (RS-5A) into strips and place them into a hat or some other container.
3. Make enough copies of "Media Helps for Our Home" (RS-5B) for everyone in the group.
4. Have extra copies of "Kids and the Media" (RS-4C) that you handed out last week for at-home reading.

❶ Our Children— the Media Addicts

Objective:
To determine the characteristics of "culturally relevant, media-oriented children" and to see whether our kids have any of those characteristics (10 minutes).

Divide the participants into three groups. Hand each group a large piece of newsprint or butcher paper. Everyone will have the same assignment.

Children who have been extensively influenced by the cultural messages displayed by the media might be called "culturally relevant, media-oriented children." Develop a list of a least five descriptive qualities of the "culturally relevant, media-oriented child." (Hints: knows a lot about the contemporary music scene, uses the right slang expressions, wants to dress according to the latest styles, spends most leisure time with the electronic media on, can mimic many media artists, has seen the latest movies, etc.)

After the groups have developed their lists of qualities, have them draw a creative picture of their "culturally relevant, media-oriented child" which portrays each of the five qualities listed. (Example: a head shaped like a television, ears that look like earphones, baggy trousers with money coming out of the pockets, the "right" foot gear, etc.) Have each group present its list of qualities and picture to the entire class.

Now, ask the group to imagine a continuum from "1" to "10" across the length of the room. On the continuum, "1" represents a child who is influenced very little by the media, and "10" represents the child who is influenced greatly by the media. Ask parents whether their children would be closer to a "1," a "10," or somewhere in between. Parents with more than one child can choose one child to represent. Have the parents notice responses of the other members of their small groups.

What do you think the position you chose on the continuum says about your children and how they are influenced by the media? (Have the parents discuss their responses in their small groups.)

"Hollywood's persistent hostility to religious values is not just peculiar, it is positively pathological."

❷ Hollywood vs. God's Commandments

Objective:
To explore whether the media violates any of the Ten Commandments (10-15 minutes).

Some argue that the Ten Commandments are the basis of our laws and social rules of conduct. But we have veered from God's instructions. Presently, in our society, there is a loosely structured moral code in operation, but it doesn't all necessarily reflect God's moral code. The ungodly code glorifies violence, lack of honesty, disobedience, hatred, racial strife, sexual sins . . . the list goes on and on.

The media sends messages. Do those messages promote what Christians believe, or take a neutral or negative stand towards our belief system? Film critic Michael Medved believes Hollywood is hostile to religion and its values. Writing in *Hollywood vs. America,* he states:

> Hollywood's persistent hostility to religious values is not just peculiar, it is positively pathological. Rather than readjusting their view of reality in order to come to terms with the religious revival in America . . . most people in the movie capital simply choose to ignore what the surveys tell them. They retreat ever deeper into their precious and hermetically sealed little world of Malibu "enlightenment," and continue to write off all religious believers as so many slope-browed bumpkins who get their clothes from K-Mart and their ideas from the *National Enquirer.*[1]

This is a stinging indictment from a Hollywood, media insider who is not himself a Christian but Jewish. His insights help explain why Christians find the messages of the media so disturbing. We should be concerned about the negative impact on our children.

Ask six volunteers (who feel they are fairly media astute) to form two teams of three. Have them sit in chairs on either side of you facing the rest of the participants. Announce a new game show called, "I've Seen It; I've Watched It; I've Played It."

Place the cut-up work sheet, "Hollywood vs. God's Commandments" (RS-5A), into a hat or some other container. As game show host, reach into the container and pick out one of the pieces of paper. Read it to the contestants.

For example, God says, **"You shall have no other gods**

before me," (Exodus 20:3), **and "Worship the Lord your god and serve him only,"** (Matthew 4:10). **Then ask the** contestants: **Where have you seen or heard this message VIOLATED in today's media in the past six months?"**

Anyone on either of the teams can yell out, "I've seen it," or "I've watched it," or "I've played it" and give an example.

The examples can come from any area of media, something visual (ads, movies, sitcoms, commercials, etc.), something audio (music, talk radio, etc.) or something played (video, party or board games, etc.). But the example must be specific. It can't be, "Oh, I hear stuff like that all the time."

Also, the example must fit the phrase they call out. If they yell out "I've seen it," then the example must pertain to something they saw, not just listened to. The audience is the judge. If the audience agrees it is a good example, give that team a point. If the audience feels it isn't a good example deduct a point. If a team provides a bad example, the other team can try to gain a point by supplying a more relevant one. The first team to earn five points wins.

Conclude the exercise by reading the following quote from H. Stephen Glenn, a youth ministry speaker. He writes about children and the media in his book, *Raising Self-Reliant Children in a Self-Indulgent World.*

> **For the first time in history, a generation of young Americans is receiving its impression about life passively from the media rather than from hands-on involvement with relevant activities. . . .**
>
> **Essentially, there are five premises portrayed over and over. The first theme is that drinking or substance abuse is the primary activity in productive social relationships. . . . The second premise is that self-medication is the primary means of eradicating pain, discomfort, and boredom. . . . The third premise is that casual sexuality is the accepted norm. . . . The fourth premise conveyed by television is that acts of violence and lawlessness are acceptable solutions to problems. . . . The fifth premise is acted out primarily in commercials. It says that patience, deferred gratification, personal initiative, and hard work are unacceptable activities.[2]**

S ome (rappers) are positive and try to instill moral values and positive messages to our children.

❸ Who Is the Media Targeting in Your Community?

Objective:
To examine the media's negative influence particularly in the local community (10-15 minutes).

Ask: **In what ways do the media target youth?**

Offer the following observations if the discussion needs some stimulation.

All youth—(There are increasing numbers of television programs and movies presented from the perspective of children or teens. Parents and authority figures are often portrayed negatively.)

Inner-city youth—(The inner-city community has been targeted by alcohol and cigarette companies. A disproportionate number of billboards are on display.

Ministers like Father Clements in the Chicago area have painted over alcohol and cigarette billboards in an attempt to force advertisers to take them down. In one court case the judge ruled in the religious leader's favor. The judge said it was an unfair practice to saturate communities of color with alcohol and cigarette advertisements.)

African-American youth—(In the sixties and seventies, several black leaders spoke out against black-exploitative movies. But the movie makers seemed interested only in making money. They didn't care about the negative messages sent to the youth and the bad image it reflected on the African-American community.

Bob Whitt, III, Director of Riverwoods Christian Center, who runs an effective program for youth, says, "The music industry has found a money maker in our young black rappers. They are not concerned about the destructive messages or about the young rapper. The music industry will use whatever makes money.")

What strategies can be used to stop the media's negative influences from dominating our children's lives? After you have allowed the group to brainstorm, add these suggestions as needed.

(Not all rappers are pushing bad messages. Some are positive and try to instill moral values and positive messages to our children. Consider positive rappers like MC Hammer, Public Enemy, Queen Latifah, X-Clan, KRS-One, and Boogie Down Productions. Some of these groups rap about Jesus, African-American history, getting jobs, and cleaning up bad language.

Boycott the negative rappers and not allow our children to buy or listen to their messages. Negative rappers include Niggers with an Attitude, Bitches with Problems, Hoes with

Attitudes, American Made Gangsters, and Two Live Crew. These rappers put down black women, encourage breaking the law and violent behaviors. The language and negative phrases they use should not be something you want plugged into your child's ears.

Join ranks with leaders who are trying to rid our communities of negative images and ask what you can do.

Comment on negative billboards as you drive through the city. Or read through magazines and listen to some of the music on the radio and discuss with your children what they are seeing and hearing.

Find posters with positive, encouraging messages and put them up in places your children frequent.)

Jawanza Kunjufu, an African-American educator, makes this comment about the media and how it's shaping the values of black youth.

At some point we're going to have to acknowledge that 72,000 hours of television—which shows 200,000 acts of violence and 25,000 sexual encounters outside of marriage—purchasing 40 percent of all movie tickets (among that group 72 percent of those purchases made by African-American youth), watching an average of 10 hours of videos a week and listening to 20 hours of rap, the billions of dollars spent advertising liquor and cigarettes on billboards, and over 10 billion dollars spent on an ad budget between television, radio, and print has to have some effect on shaping our values.[3]

As Christian parents we have a double job to do. We are trying to teach our children to have a positive view of themselves and youth of all other races, even though the media subtly and overtly communicates condescending messages about some races. As Christians, we are attempting to help our kids understand the importance of a Christ-centered life. While the media ignores Christ or puts Him down, Christian parents can not afford to be passive in this area.

Emphasize that parents can make a difference in the lives of their children in terms of the impact the media has on them.

❹ Media Touches Our Kids

Objective:
To examine what the media is saying about today's kids (10-15 minutes).

Ask the parents to get out their copies of "Kids and the Media" (RS-4C). For those who did not get a copy last week or left it at home, provide extra copies. Ask for their reactions to the information: **Were you surprised? What did you learn? How did you feel as you read the material?**

Remind the participants that the subject of the media and children could be a whole course itself. Many adults do not understand the impact of sights and sounds on our lives. This handout is designed to give the group more insight.

As time allows, read one quote at a time. For quotes that are statements of opinion, ask the participants to stand if they agree or stay in their seats if they disagree. Allow the group to choose one or two quotes they would like to discuss further. If you are leading a large group, break into smaller ones.

Conclude this activity with the following quote from *Implications* magazine.

> **Studies show that parental involvement in the listening and viewing activities of/with their children alters the media's effects upon them as young people. We must find ways to encourage and help parents to enter the music worlds of their children.**[4]

Emphasize that parents can make a difference in the lives of their children in terms of the impact the media has on them. Limiting their exposure to the media may help some, but there are other creative responses too.

❺ Getting to Work

Objective:
To help parents develop a plan for dealing with media in their families (10-15 minutes).

Media can be the conduit of all kinds of messages. The media is glamorizing unholy activities. Christians do not want their children thinking that rape, shooting, robbery, blasphemous speech, etc. is "cool!" But they often have very little idea of what to do.

Ask the group to suggest and discuss several drastic solutions one might try to take in dealing with the media problem in our families. (Demanding the children never attend another movie; locking the television in the basement; destroying every CD your child owns, etc.)

Why might these kinds of solutions be ineffective or have a backlash? (They could encourage rebellion. The children might resort to going to other people's homes to watch or listen to media—where the parents would have less control over the content. A blanket "No!" to media may take the emphasis off the importance of being discerning about content and place it on the form of communication instead.)

What are some suggestions or guidelines for developing a media policy in our families? Ask the participants to suggest ideas that are scriptural, practical, and realistic. List their suggestions on the board. Indicate the age level to which each applies by using these symbols:

✔ = preschool
✗ = grade school
★ = junior high or middle school
? = high school

Pass out "Media Controls for Our Home" (RS-5B) for some additional ideas. If time permits, give the group an opportunity to fill out the last question on the bottom of "Media Helps for Our Home" (RS-5B).

Note that what children want most is time and attention from parents. **Someone has said, "For a child, time is love." If we offer to take our children for a walk, play a game with them, help them with a project, or even offer to clean their room together with them, we would be surprised at how quickly the television is turned off, the ear plugs come out, and the magazine is put down.**

Close in prayer asking God for wisdom in selecting the most helpful responses for combating the negative influences of the media.

Notes:

1. Michael Medved, *Hollywood vs. America: Popular Culture and the War on Traditional Values* (San Francisco: Harper Collins and Grand Rapids, Mich.: Zondervan, 1992), 72.

2. Stephen Glenn, *Raising Self-Reliant Children in a Self-Indulgent World* (Rocklin, Calif.: Prima Publishing & Communications, 1989), 42.

3. Jawanza Kunjufu, *Hip-Hop vs. MAAT* (Chicago, Ill.: African American Images, 1993), 73.

4. Center for Youth Studies, Gordon Conwell Theological Seminary/ Young Life *Implications* magazine, Summer 1989, 9.

I Think My Child Is in a Gang

6

Session Aim:
To help parents identify and deal with gang activity.

Everybody calls me C.J. My mother works a lot, so my grandparents are raising me. My grandfather was the love of my life. He died a couple of years ago when I was in seventh grade. That's when all the trouble started. I started skipping classes, and destroying public property. My favorite pastime was seeing how much I could steal out of a store each day.

I'm in high school now. I spend most of my time on the streets hanging out. A couple of years ago some girls asked me to be a part of their gang. I attended a meeting. Before I knew it, I had on a Starter jacket, and I started dealing drugs. They also gave me a .38 automatic pistol which I carry in my pocket, and I know how to use it.

I always have plenty of money from the drug deals I make, and I have all the clothes I ever wanted. I really don't like being in a gang, but I don't know what else to do. Things are bad at home, and my mother doesn't have time for me. The snobbish kids at school hate me, and I don't want to go back there. The gang is the only place I feel secure and wanted.

—*Carolyn Joyce* *

*Name has been changed.

"The gang is the only place I feel secure and wanted."

Getting Ready

Scriptures:
Matthew 11:28-30; 12:46-50;
17:20; 28:20b; Mark 9:36, 37;
Luke 4:18, 19; 11:9-13;
12:25-32; Jeremiah 9:17-21.

1. Make enough photocopies of "Facts and Figures about Gangs" (RS-6A), "Gang Identifiers" (RS-6B), and "What Can We Do?" (RS-6C) for everyone.
2. Make an extra copy of "What Can We Do?" (RS-6C) and cut apart the three situations only to use in Step 3.

❶ Looking at the Outside

Objective:
To help parents become familiar with gangs and identify their symbols (10-15 minutes).

Give each person a blank piece of paper and pencil. Ask the participants to answer true or false to questions as you read them from "Facts and Figures about Gangs" (RS-6A). After you have finished, pass out the resource sheet and go over the answers. Ask: **What facts surprised you? Why?**

Have participants turn over "Facts and Figures about Gangs" and use the back to draw a picture of what they think a gang member looks like. They don't have to be good artists. Just encourage them to include as many specific details as possible. After the participants have completed their pictures, pass out copies of "Gang Identifiers" (RS-6B). Tell them to give themselves a point for each identifier they included in their picture. Applaud the ones with the most specific points.

What experience have you had with gang activity? (Some participants may have been involved in a gang when they were younger. Others may have children in one now. They may encounter gang members or their families professionally by reason of being law enforcement officers, social workers, teachers, etc.) Encourage them to share helpful information about gangs in your area during the sessions. Limit the length of sharing according to your available time.

❷ What's Going on Inside?

Objective:
To help parents understand the internal thinking of a gang member (15 minutes).

Now that we've looked at a gang member on the outside, let's examine his or her inner thinking. Go around the room asking the participants for descriptive words to identify the inner feelings or thinking of a member of a gang or a youth thinking about joining one. Write these words on the board in a column to the left. Divide the group into four teams. Assign each team a pair of Scripture references.

Team 1—Matthew 12:46-50 and Matthew 28:20b
Team 2—Matthew 11:28-30 and Matthew 17:20
Team 3—Mark 9:36, 37 and Luke 4:18, 19
Team 4—Luke 11:9-13 and Luke 12:25-32

et's not forget that the gang member's deepest need is the Lord Jesus Christ.

Say: **Look up your verses and see how they might apply to the inner feelings of gang members. For each one, write down the feeling, the verse, and a phrase stating how Christ understands and helps satisfy that deep longing.**

When the teams have finished, have the group come back and share their responses. Try to match the Scriptures with the words on the board. Keep this list for reference in Step 4. Your list may look something like this:

Feeling	Verse(s)	How Christ Helps
Loneliness	Matthew 12:46-50	Christ becomes a brother.
	Matthew 28:20b	Christ is always with us.
Confusion Anger	Matthew 11:28-30	Christ give us rest from our anxieties.
Hopelessness	Matthew 17:20	Christ can do the impossible for us.
Rejection	Mark 9:36, 37	Christ welcomes us.
Guilt	Luke 4:18, 19	Christ frees and heals us.
Greed	Luke 11:9-13 Luke 12:25-32	Christ supplies our needs.

As the gang problem is analyzed, let's not forget that the gang member's deepest need is the Lord Jesus Christ. Christ alone can heal, forgive, and transform a life. He alone has the power to help our youth withstand the seemingly irresistible temptations of money, fame, power, and a need to belong. Have group members tell how they share their faith with young people at home or in the community.

Ask: **How strong is the youth evangelism program of the church?** Encourage the parents to talk about the church's youth program, but do not end on a note of criticism. Throw it back to the participants who, as concerned members, can make a difference.

Who is behind the gang and drug problem in our country? (Mafia, corrupt politicians, unscrupulous businessmen, etc. The bottom line is money.)

Gangs are a symptom of a larger problem—SIN.

Acknowledge that there are some corrupt people in high places or positions of power who allow drugs to be brought into the country and then label gangs as THE problem. Not so. Gangs are a symptom of a larger problem—SIN. Point out that those who are behind the scenes are receiving big profits by preying on our young people. They use the lure of money and desire to belong to draw very young boys and girls into a life of violence and crime. Encourage group members to pray for victory over these forces of evil.

❸ What Can Be Done?

Objective:
To give parents practical suggestions about gang activity (15-20 minutes).

Regroup into three teams. Give each team paper, pens, and a different situation from the cut-apart copy of "What Can We Do?" (RS-6C). Assign each team to counsel and advise the person(s) in their particular situation. NOTE: DO NOT give them the suggestions printed under each situation at this time.

Reunite the whole group and review the situations, inviting the teams to share their counsel. Regulate the length of discussion according to your available time. After discussing each team's counsel, hand out complete copies of "What Can We Do?" (RS-6C) for more suggestions and information.

❹ Using a Powerful Tool to Deal with the Gang Problem

Objective:
To help and encourage participants to seriously pray about the gang problem (5-10 minutes).

Ask: **What do you think will happen in this country if gang activity continues to increase?** After group responses, share the following observations from *Gangs in America* by Wendell Amstutz and Bart Larson[1] :

- **Increased violence. Possible civil war between ethnic groups.**
- **Thousands of children, teen, and adult drug addicts.**
- **AIDS could claim thousands of adolescents and young adults.**
- **Neighborhoods becoming war zones.**
- **Anarchy as police become outnumbered.**
- **Jails and prisons unable to hold all drug offenders.**
- **City, state, and national budgets stretched beyondlimits.**
- **Whole ethnic groups wiped out.**

Wendell Amstutz and Bart Larson say, "This younger

oneliness, despair, hopelessness, and debt are doing their damage in our families."

generation is angry and mean. Things have changed a lot since crack hit the streets."[2]

Ask parents to think of someone they know who is actually struggling with the kind of situations described in RS-6C. This person might be in their own household, community, or church. Be sensitive to anyone who is personally struggling.

Tell them to close their eyes as you read Jeremiah 9:17-21 and this quote from *Chosen Vessels*, by Rebecca Osaigbovo, who is leading a major prayer campaign for our cities.

> **Why is there a need for such urgency, intensity and confession? "Death is come up into our windows, and is entered into our palaces, to cut off the children from without, and young men from the streets." Sounds like our urban areas today: Cocaine, alcohol, promiscuous lifestyles, suicide, violence, the New Age movement, gangs, homosexuality, and much more are swallowing up our youth, our children. Loneliness, despair, hopelessness, and debt are doing their damage in our families.**
>
> **Is death coming into our windows to cut off the children? What will it take before we make haste to pray with an intensity that is beyond our normal supplications?**
>
> **These are our sons, nephews, daughters, nieces, granddaughters, grandsons, and neighbors. Do we sit idly by and let them be picked off one by one?[3]**

Encourage parents by referring to the list of Feelings, Verses, and How Christ Helps you developed in Step 2.

Close in prayer for the children and parents who are caught in the violence of the streets.

Notes:

1. Wendell Amstutz and Bart Larson, *Gangs in America* (Rochester, Minn.: National Counseling Resource, 1993), 93-95.

2. Ibid.

3. Rebecca Osaigbovo, *Chosen Vessels* (Detroit, Mich.: DaBar Services, 1991), 155, 156.

What Puts Dion (or Darla) 7 "At-Risk?"

In this session you will be introduced to a boy named Dion (or it could be a girl named Darla). Dion is "at risk." This means he is often in some kind of trouble.

At-risk kids like Dion are not a new phenomenon. Remember Fat Albert and the Cosby kids? How about the Li'l Rascals and Fonzie from "Happy Days?" Hollywood writers and novelists have turned some at-risk behaviors into entertaining scenarios.

You will find at-risk kids like Dion in the Bible, also. The activities of the prodigal son probably raised a few eyebrows in his neighborhood. And did you ever wonder why James and John were called "Sons of Thunder?" Were they perhaps troublemakers?

However, the at-risk Dions and Darlas we meet today are not interesting biblical characters or amusing television stars. They are juvenile delinquents, troublemakers, misfits, gang-bangers, and skinheads. They live in posh suburban areas, farming communities, and low-income urban centers. Unfortunately, their activities are not precocious adventures or harmless pranks. Most twentieth-century at-risk youngsters are in deep trouble, making big mistakes, and scarring themselves for life.

Usually, an at-risk youth is easy to spot, unless he or she happens to be living in your home. Sentiment can sometimes cause a parent to put blinders on and make excuses for some pretty uncivilized behavior.

Sentiment can sometimes cause a parent to put blinders on and make excuses for some pretty uncivilized behavior.

Getting Ready

Scriptures:
II Samuel 13:1, 8-14, 21-29, 37-39; 14:21-33; 15:1-10, 13, 14; 18:9-15, 33.

1. Photocopy enough copies for everyone of "Warning Signs" (RS-7A).
2. Calculate how many teams of no more than four people your group would make. Then make as many copies of "The Life of Absalom" (RS-7B) as you will have teams. (Make a few extra copies in case participants want intact copies later.) Cut apart a sheet for each team as indicated and place the strips plus the top of the resource sheet in an envelope, and number the envelope. Each team will get an envelope with a complete cut-apart sheet in it.
3. Prepare enough copies of "Could My Child Turn Out Like Dion?" (RS-7C) so that parents may complete one for each child.

❶ Meet At-Risk Dion

Objective:
To help parents discover indicators of at-risk behavior (10-20 minutes).

Hand out the work sheet "Warning Signs" (RS-7A). Ask participants to read through the list of behaviors that a variety of experts have determined may be indicators of potential problems. Then read—or have a volunteer read—the following case study of Dion. When you are finished, have participants check off on their work sheet the at-risk behaviors Dion is exhibiting.

Dion is fourteen years old. He lives in a large city. Like many communities, it is diverse economically, ethnically, and racially.

He should be a freshman in high school, but was held back in fifth grade so he could work on basic skills. Even though he is very bright, teachers are concerned that he doesn't take school seriously. He only uses a limited portion of his potential. Dion shrugs his shoulders and says, "I don't care," when he is questioned about his school performance. He's been absent quite a bit lately.

Dion was an all-star Little League player in seventh grade but has decided not to play in eighth grade or high school. Dion says, "All the coaches I know are stupid. They never let people play the game the right way."

Dion and his parents attended church regularly at one time, but Dion's dad got into an argument with the minister, and they quit attending. They don't even go to church on Easter or Christmas anymore.

Dion has a girlfriend. They are sexually active. Dion doesn't use a condom. He's afraid his friends might make fun of him if they found out. He says, "I'm not concerned about my girl friend getting pregnant. If she does, there are ways of taking care of it."

Dion's friends used to be the kids in his immediate neighborhood. But in the past year, he began to hang out with some older kids, several blocks away. Whenever he is with his new friends, he wears a certain kind of clothes and certain colors. When Dion's new friends call, they don't ask for him by name; they ask for "Boogie." Dion says, "Don't worry, it's just a nickname. It doesn't mean anything."

Dion spends his evenings with those friends. On weekends, he rarely comes home. His mother and father say, "We just can't control his coming and going anymore."

Last summer, Dion's parents were called to the police station. The police thought Dion was involved in some illegal activity. The police didn't have any proof, but wanted to alert the parents. Dion's father got into a shouting match with the sergeant. He was angry because the sergeant made them come down to the station when they had no concrete charges. "After all," Dion's father said, "I don't need the police telling me how to raise my kid."

That night Dion's father warned him to stay away from his "goofball friends." Father and son got into a yelling match, and his father slapped Dion around until Dion hit his father in the stomach with one of his new karate moves and told his father never to touch him again.

The music Dion listens to has a rebellious tone. His mother read in the newspaper that his favorite group advocated beating up your girlfriend and raping her if you wanted to. When she asked Dion about it, he said, "I don't even pay any attention to what they are saying. I just like listening to the beat and dancing to it."

Dion doesn't work, but he and his buddies always seem to have plenty of money. He smokes cigarettes now. Quite often, Dion's mother thinks there is a marijuana odor on his clothing.

Dion's mother found photos of Dion and his new friends. They were all making strange signs with their hands. Dion says "Uh, don't worry, Mom. We're just friends goofing around."

After you have allowed the participants time to check off indicators of potential problems on their work sheets, ask the following questions.

What is Dion at-risk for, or in other words, what could his behavior be leading to? (Dion is at-risk for dropping out of school, fathering a child out of wedlock, gang activity, unlawful activities, drug dependency, violence, etc.)

What behaviors may be indicative of approaching violence? (Father is violent with him, and he responded in kind. Drugs and gang activity may be involved. He is not bothered by lyrics advocating violence.)

If you are leading an hour-long session, divide the group into several teams. (Otherwise, go on to Step 2.) Ask teams to come up with what might make a difference in Dion's life. Acknowledge that at-risk kids often need help of many kinds. Most importantly, they need the hope that comes from new life in Christ.

❷ Observing an At-Risk Dion in the Bible

Objective:
To help parents understand the danger of ignoring at-risk indicators (10 minutes).

Have the participants divide up into teams of about four people each. Give each team an envelope containing the cut-apart resource sheet, "The Life of Absalom" (RS-7B), according to the instructions in the Getting Ready section of this session. Conduct a contest to see which team can most quickly unscramble Absalom's life by arranging the strips in chronological order. Remind the teams that if they are unfamiliar with this Bible story, they may use the Bible passages listed on the top of the resource sheet.

The following is the correct order:

1. Absalom's sister Tamar is raped by their stepbrother Amnon, one of David's son's (II Sam. 13:1, 8-14).

2. David heard about the rape, and he was angry, but did nothing about it (II Sam. 13:21).

3. Absalom said nothing to Amnon after the rape of his sister, but two years later he had Amnon killed to avenge the raping of his sister (II Sam. 13:22-29).

4. Absalom fled after killing Amnon, and went to Geshur (where his mother's father and relatives lived), and David mourned for his son every day, but did nothing (II Sam. 13:37-39).

5. David sent for Absalom to return from Geshur to Jerusalem, but David took a long time to forgive Absalom and didn't want to see him. Absalom lived in Jerusalem for two years before David allowed him to come see him (II Sam. 14:21-33).

6. After seeing David, Absalom still rebelled and got several men to follow him. He revolted against his father and ran David out of the city and made himself king (II Sam. 15:1-10; 13, 14).

7. David's men pursued Absalom to restore David to the throne. They found Absalom hanging from a tree. He was then killed as he hung from the tree (II Sam. 18:9-15).

8. David wept bitterly and mourned the death of his son (II Sam. 18:33).

After the story is unscrambled, ask:

Why would Absalom be considered an at-risk child? (He was violent, rebellious, angry, revengeful, and undisciplined; he did not have a good home life; etc.)

How did his father contribute to his negative behavior? (He would not forgive him, would not communicate with him, and was not attentive to his son's concerns and needs.)

Why is it unwise for parents to ignore negative behavior? (Overlooking at-risk behavior could lead to worse behavior or deadly consequences, fragment the family, cause everyone to suffer and other problems.)

What are some elements that could have been introduced into Absalom's life that might have kept him from such a tragic end? (His father could have taken time to help

Absalom understand spiritual truths. Someone else could have been there for Absalom to talk to when David wasn't available. He could have turned to God for forgiveness and help.)

❸ Could My Child Turn Out Like Dion?

Objective:
To allow parents to evaluate their own children in light of at-risk behaviors (10 minutes).

Ask participants to fill out a copy of "Could My Child Turn Out Like Dion?" (RS-7C) for each of their children, then answer the questions at the bottom. Encourage parents to be very honest in their evaluation and open to what God reveals.

❹ Let's Help Dion

Objective:
To identify factors that might give Dion a second chance (15-20 minutes).

Assure the group that the scenario about Dion's future does not have to come true. If other factors are introduced into Dion's life at this point, Dion may be able to beat the odds. Remember to give participants encouragement throughout this process. Hopefully, very few people in your group will have a "Dion or Darla" in their home. However, some participants may be seeing enough negative indicators in their children's life to seriously worry them.

What causes children to turn out like Dion? Perhaps if we can understand some of the factors that contribute to at-risk behavior, we can take steps to deal with them. There are no easy answers. Kids from great families develop at-risk tendencies while other kids from horrible homes seem to do well. Sometimes kids from stable homes commit violent acts at the same time kids who aren't sure who Dad is and are being raised by an incompetent mother end up going to Harvard and making positive contributions. The home situation is a major factor, but not the only ingredient.

However, while there are no formulas or magic keys, there is growing evidence of the causes of at-risk behavior. Here are three reasons why Dion is at-risk:

1. **Dion has no relationship with Jesus Christ.**
2. **Dion lacks some basic skills and perceptions about himself that are needed to make him an effective person.**

3. Dion has a home life that is up for grabs.

Explain that the next activity is to "help" Dion and his parents. He has been arrested for petty theft. Have the group imagine that they have been invited to offer some help to Dion and his family in the form of letters. Form four teams, and give these assignments:

Team 1: Write Dion about becoming a Christian.
Team 2: Write and help Dion change his negative perception about himself and the circumstances in his life.
Team 3: Encourage Dion about his home life and offer alternatives to help.
Team 4: Write a letter to Dion's parents suggesting ways that they might help Dion.

Encourage each group to use at least one Scripture passage in the letter. They should keep in mind that Dion is only fourteen. The letters should be short, to the point, and not preach at him. (Possible Scriptures: Team 1—John 1:12; Team 2—I Cor. 10:13; Team 3—Ps. 103; Team 4—Prov. 22:6.)

After five or ten minutes, have the groups reconvene and share their letters.

After Team 1 reads its letter encouraging Dion to become a become a Christian, share the following comment by Gordon McLean, a Christian youth worker, particularly experienced in working with gang members.

I spoke at a Chicago conference sponsored by law enforcement and neighborhood groups offering ways to deal with the gangs and was introduced by the words, "Now we will have Mr. McLean discuss the religious option." That really got to me, so I grabbed the microphone and said, "We are not just another option; we are all there is!" What I meant was that unless God did a miracle in a kid's life, remaking him from the inside out, then every other community effort to solve the problems of youth violence was found to fail. Education, family counseling, recreation, law enforcement, job training— all are good and important in their place but never a substitute for spiritual rebirth.[1]

After Team 2 shares its letter encouraging Dion's self-perception and outlook on life, read the following.

In his book, *Raising Self-Reliant Children in a Self-Indulgent World,* **H. Stephen Glenn says that for at-risk young people to become low-risk individuals they need to develop** *strong . . .*

1. **Perceptions of personal capabilities: "I am capable."**
2. **Perceptions of significance in primary relationships: "I contribute in meaningful ways and I am genuinely needed."**
3. **Perceptions of personal power or influence over life: "I can influence what happens to me."**
4. **Intrapersonal skills: The ability to understand personal emotions, use that understanding to develop self-discipline and self-control, and learn from experience.**
5. **Interpersonal skills: The ability to work with others and develop friendships through communication, cooperation, negotiation, sharing, empathizing, and listening.**
6. **Systematic skills: The ability to respond to the limits and consequences of everyday life with responsibility, adaptability, flexibility, and integrity.**
7. **Judgment skills: The ability to use wisdom and evaluate situations according to appropriate values.**[2]

After Teams 3 and 4 read their letters about Dion's home life, make this comment: **When "home" is a rocky place, it's hard on children. Kids who have a good, strong home where they feel safe and secure, deal with a violent, upside-down world more effectively than children who don't. It's never too late to start smoothing out the bumps in a rocky home life. No matter how bad it looks, you can take a step in another direction. It's a step worth taking. In fact, it's the only step worth taking.**

Before closing in prayer ask the participants to think of one plan of action they can put into practice this week to nurture or strengthen their child. Challenge them to pray specifically for that area.

Close by having couples pray with each other. If there are single parents, have them form pairs or triads.

Notes:

1. Gordon McLean with Dave and Neta Jackson, *Cities of Lonesome Fear* (Chicago: Moody, 1993), 75.
2. H. Stephen Glenn and Jane Nelsen, *Raising Self-Reliant Children in a Self-Indulgent World* (Rocklin, Calif: Prima Publishing and Communications, 1989), 49, 50.

Making Our Families Stronger

8

Session Aim:
To help parents understand how to build a strong family unit which can combat violence.

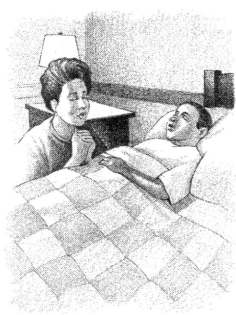

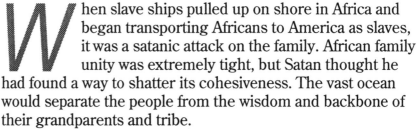

When slave ships pulled up on shore in Africa and began transporting Africans to America as slaves, it was a satanic attack on the family. African family unity was extremely tight, but Satan thought he had found a way to shatter its cohesiveness. The vast ocean would separate the people from the wisdom and backbone of their grandparents and tribe.

The security and love of father and mother were thousands of miles away. The power in a band of brothers, sisters, uncles, aunts, and cousins was splintered across the southern states. A lonely young African girl stood on the auction block waiting to be sold into the cruel realities of slavery.

And yet, the African-American family has survived. I still see the scene from *Roots* when Kizzy, the daughter of Kunta Kenta, was sold to a sex-hungry slave master. The mother stretched out on the ground, weeping, pleading, and reaching for her child.

I sit in women's prayer groups today and listen to mothers praying for their families, stretched out before an almighty God: "Lord, please don't let Satan destroy my family . . . my husband . . . my child." God is listening. God is working. God has His loving, strong arms around the fragmented pieces of our family. He always has, and He always will.

—Victoria Johnson

***G**od has His loving, strong arms around the fragmented pieces of our family. He always has, and He always will.*

Getting Ready

Scriptures:
Luke 15:11-32.

1. Have the following questions written on a board or newsprint when the class begins. Cover the questions with something until you are ready to use them.
   - How is the family in these Scriptures like some families today?
   - How is the family unlike some families today?
   - Why do you think Jesus used the family unit as the primary setting for this important teaching?
   - What are the strengths of this family?
   - What are its weaknesses?
   - What do you think Jesus was trying to teach us about God's family?
2. Put up six paper banners around the room. Each banner should have a separate heading and plenty of room to write below it. The banner headings should be as follows:
   - Commitment to the Family
   - Spend Time Together
   - Have Good Family Communication
   - Express Appreciation to Each Other
   - Have a Spiritual Commitment
   - Able to Solve Problems in a Crisis
3. Photocopy "The Prodigal Son Improv" (RS-8A) and "Looking at the Strength of Our Family" (RS-8B) for each group member.

❶ The Positive Side of Our Family

Objective:
To examine the strength of the our family (10 minutes).

So much attention is given to the negative aspects of family life. Let's take time and reflect on what's encouraging and positive about the family unit. Think about the family you were raised in. What was good about it? What are lessons that were established in your family that are still with you today? What's the positive side of the family? List the responses on the board in single words or short phrases. Your list might include things like: (Togetherness; sense of identity; dependable, strong; loyalty; fun; creativity; resilience; loving; close-knit; resourceful; flexible.)

Leave the list on the board as you share the following thoughts: **There is a debate raging in our society about how to define the family. On one extreme is the position that the two-parent family is a thing of the past. At the other end of the spectrum is God's standard: A mother and father who are committed to each other and their** children for life. It is important that children see this as the desired way to experience family life.

At the same time, we must acknowledge that many children will spend at least some time in a single-parent family. Many others will never know their biological fathers. Single parents and their children need to know that God can and will be "a father to the fatherless" (Ps. 68:5).

Point out that the purpose of this session is to focus on how any family can be strengthened.

❷ The Family . . . God Knows What He's Doing

Objective:
To examine the story of the prodigal son to emphasize God's high view of the family (10-25 minutes).

If your session is only forty-five minutes long, have someone read Luke 15:11-32 and move on to discuss the questions. Otherwise do "The Prodigal Son Improv."

Pass out copies of "The Prodigal Son Improv" (RS-8A) and divide your group into four dramatic teams. Assign each team to portray one of the scenes in a different dramatic style. Let the groups go over their scene description briefly and select the style of their choice provided no other team has chosen the same style. That is, first-come-first-served on the style selections. Then give the teams about five minutes to plan how they are going to act out their scene. It will be primarily an improvisation, so no rehearsal and only limited planning should be needed. Tell the teams that they have only three minutes to portray their scene. Make sure to keep the activities in this step moving rapidly.

Encourage everyone to have a lot of fun with this and to ham it up! Suggest the use of exaggerated accents and actions within their styles. Group members should consult Luke 15:11-32 for additional details to the story.

After the improv or the reading of the passage, discuss the following questions.

How is the family in these Scriptures like some families today? (Rebellious children, faithful children, jealousy in the families, thinking that partying and having a good time are the most important things in the world.)

How is the family unlike some families today? (Forgiveness, peacemaking family, father has a predominant role and wise actions.)

Why do you think Jesus uses the family unit as the primary setting for this important teaching? (The family is important to Him, to teach family principles, to show us how the family is supposed to reflect God's relationship with us.)

What are the strengths of this family? (Wealth, forgiveness, a wise father.)

What are the weaknesses of this family? (Father may not have given the older son enough recognition, there was jealousy, the older son was not compassionate about his brother, perhaps the father was too generous.)

What do you think Jesus was trying to teach us about God's family? (How much our heavenly Father unconditionally loves us, God will always take us back. The family on earth is to reflect His family in heaven.)

Satan's attacks on the family are relentless. If he cannot destroy it by external means, he will attack from within. For example, he tried to destroy the black family with slavery. Even so, the strength of the black family prevailed and at one time it modeled many strengths to other families in America. The extended family dominated the neighborhoods, children were taken in if their natural family needed help, marriage and children were held in high regard, the elderly were respected, and the church was the social center. The African-American family has been hit hard in recent years by violence, drugs, divorce, and poverty, but God has allowed it to continue to stand. Hispanic, Asian, Caucasian, and all other families have experienced similar attacks. What is needed to strengthen families in America?

❸ A Strong Family Is within Reach

Objective:
To look at the six strengths of strong families (15 minutes).

Chuck Swindoll sheds some light on this question in his book, *The Strong Family*. Listen to what he says:

My research confirms two findings: 1. A fulfilling and happy family is as strong today as it was fifty years ago—maybe even stronger, and 2. effective family life does not just happen; it is the result of deliberate intention, determination and practice. . . . Not much research is done on strong, happy families. Most professional authorities focus their attention on families that are fractured by internal struggles.

Professor Nick Stinnett is an exception. Dr. Stinnett . . . launched a fascinating "family strengths research project." . . . His study included strong black families as well as white, strong ethnic families, and strong single-parent families. . . . There was only one criterion for being included in the sample of strong families: the families had to rate themselves very high in marriage happiness and in their satisfaction in parent-child relationships. . . . The goals? Very simply, to discover what makes families strong.

Dr. Stinnett found six main qualities in strong families. Strong families:
- are committed to the family
- spend time together
- have good family communication
- express appreciation to each other
- have a spiritual commitment
- and are able to solve problems in a crisis.[1]

Direct attention to the six banners (each with one of the six characteristics of a strong family on it) you have taped around the room. Divide the group into six teams, so there is an equal number of participants sitting under each banner. If your group is small, use three teams and have each one work on two banners. Give each team this assignment: **Your pastor will be giving a series of sermons talking about strong family life. He wants your group to help him come up with practical, realistic, but challenging ideas for how the family characteristic(s) on your banner(s) can be enhanced.** Have the teams write their ideas on the bottom part of their banners.

The next step will provide people with a chance to appreciate the creative ideas of other teams. Use the following ideas should any team need some priming. These strengths complement each other, so it's natural that some ideas appear under multiple characteristics.

Strong families are committed to the family. (Meet as a family weekly. Place a priority on doing fun things together as a family. Mom and Dad should work to keep their relationship solid. They should talk over important issues with the family in light of what certain decisions might mean for the family. Work less. Divide up family responsibilities so one person doesn't carry too much of the load.)

Strong families express appreciation . . . have a spiritual commitment . . . are able to solve problems in a crisis.

Strong families spend time together. (Meet as a family on a weekly basis. Mom and Dad schedule special time with each child each week. Take family vacations. Enjoy meals together as much as possible. Take the phone off the hook during meals. Have a game night each week. Plan fun days with the kids in charge, giving them a budget.)

Strong families have good family communication. (Meet as a family on a weekly basis. Mom and Dad schedule special time with each child each week. Develop an environment where the family focuses on solutions to problems. Emphasize time spent together interacting with less time in front of the tube. Talk with—not at—each other.)

Strong families express appreciation to each other. (Declare a "special person" day once a month, rotating it between all family members; the person gets a special meal and everyone says one positive thing about him or her. Mom and Dad write love letters to the children. Siblings attend each other's athletic, music, and drama performances and provide moral support. Ask for the children's help when doing an important task.)

Strong families have a spiritual commitment. (Mom and Dad make it a habit to pray with each child at bedtime. Have devotions at dinner time. Attend church together. Discuss important issues together in view of God's Word.)

Strong families are able to solve problems in a crisis. (Make the children part of the decision-making process. Have them work with parents in establishing rules. Parents make it a point not to deal with hard issues while they are feeling emotionally charged. Discuss potential crisis situations before they occur. Emphasize solutions; don't blame. Learn what's normal and what's a crisis.)

❹ How Does My Family Measure Up?

Objective:
To give participants an opportunity to spend some time evaluating their own families (10 minutes).

After the completed banners have been rehung, distribute copies of "Looking at the Strength of Our Family" (RS-8B) and have the participants fill them out alone.

Take a look at your family and evaluate to determine where it needs strengthening. Indicate next to "I say" how strong you think that characteristic is in your family. Indicate what you think your children might say on their line. For ideas on how to make your family stronger, walk around the room looking at the suggestions

provided on the banners of the other characteristics of strong families.

While parents are filling out the first part of the resource sheet, copy the following suggestions from Pastor Tony Evans onto the board. Let these suggestions and the banners serve as an "Idea Fair" to help the parents. Have them write ideas in the third column of the work sheet.

Below are some suggestions for how the church can assist in strengthening the family unit. If you have time, discuss them with the group members being open to their suggestions for additional ideas. You may wish to present your suggestions to the pastor.

Ten Ways the Church Can Assist the Family

- Develop strong children's programs.
- Offer child care at church services and day care during the week.
- Give marital and parental training.
- Provide Christian counseling.
- Furnish resources through a church library.
- Provide financial counseling.
- Create family-centered worship experiences.
- Schedule family-centered activities.
- Offer special help to single parents.
- Address family issues facing your community.

Conclude the session in prayer, asking several people in the group to pray: (1) thanking God for preserving the family in spite of past and present difficulties, (2) asking Him for help for individual families situations, (3) praying for our churches to become more involved in helping strengthen families.

Notes:

1. Chuck Swindoll, *The Strong Family* (Portland, Ore.: Multnomah Press, 1991), 13, 14.

2. Anthony T. Evans, *Guiding Your Family in a Misguided World,* Focus on the Family Publishing, 1991, 107-121.

Training without Provoking

9

Session Aim:
To help parents begin to develop habits of effective Christian parenting techniques.

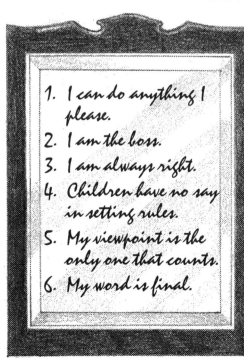

1. I can do anything I please.
2. I am the boss.
3. I am always right.
4. Children have no say in setting rules.
5. My viewpoint is the only one that counts.
6. My word is final.

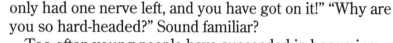

only had one nerve left, and you have got on it!" "Why are you so hard-headed?" Sound familiar?

Too often young people have succeeded in becoming the fingernails on the blackboard of their parents' lives. On the other hand, many parents have succeeded in exasperating their offspring. In some cases, this has given birth to a full-blown rebellion.

The family is the first line of defense for helping young people deal with a violent culture. But what if the family structure is impaired in some way? What if parents use communication strategies that "don't work, won't work, and shouldn't work," but insist on using them anyway? Where will young people turn?

Hopefully, they will turn to other significant adults. But if other caring adults are not present, the streets have open arms. The young person will find within those arms negative peer influence, a warped culture, gang activity, and probably violence. We've got to keep our kids out of the streets!

The only person I can control in a relationship is me."

Getting Ready:

Scriptures:
Ephesians 6:1-4;
Ecclesiastes 1:9

1. Make enough copies for everyone of "The Dirty Dozen: Parenting Strategies for an Unhappy Family" (RS-9A) and "Clarifying the Parenting Issues" (RS-9B).
2. On separate 3" x 5" cards, write out the three skit scenarios in Step 1 (see page 65).
3. Create signs to post around the room with the following words on them:
NEVER, EVER
MY KIDS WOULD SAY I DO IT ALL THE TIME
SOMETIMES, MORE THAN I'D LIKE TO ADMIT
I THINK IT A LOT, BUT I USUALLY DON'T ACT ON IT
UH-OH! THAT'S ME. LORD, FORGIVE ME !
SOUNDS A LOT LIKE MY NEIGHBOR
4. Copy the following questions on the board and, if possible, cover them until they are needed in Step 3 (see page 66).
   - Can you think of a reason why a parent might justify using this strategy?
   - When parents use this strategy what is the usual reaction of children?
   - How could using this strategy be considered violent?
5. Optional: Small prize for the group who includes the most strategies from "The Dirty Dozen" in their skit in Step 1.

❶ We're So Bad . . . We Could Be on TV

Objective:
To identify twelve parenting strategies that don't work (10-15 minutes).

Hand out the resource sheet, "The Dirty Dozen: Parenting Strategies for an Unhappy Family" (RS-10A). Ask volunteers to read aloud one "Strategy" at a time.

Allow the parents a few moments to look over the sheet as you explain that these are typical behaviors engaged in by some parents. Chances are everyone in the room has done one or more of the activities listed. These strategies are quite toxic in family relationships. The result is that family members don't trust, talk, or resolve problems. They look elsewhere for meaning and purpose. Many at-risk children will tell you these are strategies that have chased them into the street.

Sometimes parents say that their children push them or even force them into acting in negative ways at times. There is a basic rule that governs human relationships: "The only person I can control in a relationship is me." This means I still have the freedom to choose appropriate responses no matter what my child does.

Write on the board: "The only person I can control in a

relationship is me." Ask the group if they agree with this statement.

Have the participants form three groups. Announce that we have just formed the "Unhappy Family Players." Each group will act out one of the following scenarios using as many of the "Dirty Dozen" principles as possible. Give each group a 3" x 5" card with one of the following scenarios written on it:

Skit 1: Act out a typical scene between parents and children discussing a home situation where they disagree.

Skit 2: Act out a group of kids sitting around talking about their parents who use these strategies. Zero in on what they feel kids' honest reactions to these strategies might be.

Skit 3: Act out a group of parents sitting around rationalizing why they feel it's okay to use the "Dirty Dozen."

After the skits are performed for the whole group, take a vote on which skit used the most "Dirty Dozen" strategies. Optional: Give each member of the winning cast a small prize.

Keep parents in the same three groups for the next activity.

❷ Don't Provoke Them

Objective:
To discover what the Bible says about aggravating our children (10 minutes).

Read Ephesians 6:1-3, then ask: **How many of you hope and pray that your children will take this commandment to heart?** Ask for a show of hands. Most hands should go up.

Before reading Ephesians 6:4, explain to the parents: **The next verse is one that your kids are hoping and praying you will take to heart!** Read verse four aloud.

Keep participants in the same three groups, making sure each one has writing materials. Make these assignments:

Group 1: List things their parents did to aggravate them.

Group 2: List things their kids would say they do to cause aggravation.

Group 3: List kids' responses when aggravated by their parents.

Bring the three groups together again, and have them share their lists.

Rules without relationship leads to rebellion.

❸ A Closer Look

Objective:
To help parents identify their responses and discuss possible outcomes of using typical parenting strategies (15 minutes).

Read aloud the six signs you made before the session and placed around the room. Instruct the group that you will be reading "The Dirty Dozen" one at a time. As you do so, they should go to the sign that best describes their response. Once a group gathers under the sign, have them answer the three questions that you wrote on the board before group time.

- **Can you think of a reason why a parent might justify using this strategy?**
- **When parents use this strategy, what is the usual reaction of children?**
- **How could following this strategy be considered a violent act?**

❹ What We Know about Kids and What They Like

Objective:
To review basic issues regarding kids and parenting (10-20 minutes).

Parents sometimes act the way they do because they have quit being students of their children and their culture. Many people have quit growing. Here's an easy true/false test that can help clarify some important issues.

Pass out copies of "Clarifying the Parenting Issues" (RS-9B). Give parents time to indicate true or false to the statements on the resource sheet. After they have finished, go over the statements while offering the following input. As time allows, discuss each one.

1. Kids want a relationship with their parents. (*True.* Kids want parents to be available. But they don't want to be embarrassed by their parents. So, even though kids love to be able to talk to Mom and/or Dad about important issues, they sometimes behave cautiously. As kids grow older, the relationship needs to redefine itself.)

2. Rules without relationship leads to rebellion. (*True.* Think of a time when you had a rule imposed upon you. How did you react? Kids like to give their input and feel like they've had a stake in the decision making. Parents need to build relationships with their kids.)

3. Times have changed so much. Everything my kid is going through is different than what I faced. (*False.* Kids are growing up in a different world, but the most critical things don't change. As Ecclesiastes 1:9 says, "there is nothing new under the sun." You can still understand what it feels like to be gossiped about, not be picked for a game, or to be apprehensive about relationships. Circumstances change. Feelings don't. Try to remember the feelings of childhood and adolescence.)

4. Choose your battles wisely or you'll be battling all the time. (*True.* Kids can push your button in a 101 ways. Save the battle gear for the stuff that really matters.)

5. Kids are impressed when you say "When I was your age. . . ." (*False.* Kids are no more impressed when you say that than you were when your parents said the same to you.)

6. Kids will react better if they feel supported before being challenged. (*True.* Kids need to feel that they have a safe, secure, home base. Support your kids emotionally and you'll be able to challenge them in the important areas.)

7. Kids are under so much pressure, they don't need an environment filled with consequences. (*False.* Kids are under a lot of pressure because they grow up not knowing what real consequences are. However, try to make consequences naturally or logically related to the behavior so the kids will learn from their mistakes.)

8. Kids think faith is stupid. (*False.* Kids want a real faith, but it has got to be their faith. God has children, not grandchildren. As children become older, they cannot ride along on the coattails of your faith. Help your kids develop faith by modeling a godly lifestyle and by making faith a natural part of your life.)

9. The world is such a scary place that parents need to be especially strict with their kids. (*False.* Being overly strict can cause kids to rebel. Overly strict parents don't involve children in the decision-making process. The result is that the rules established appear arbitrary and unfair. Unless you plan on making every decision for your child the rest of his or her life you need to equip him or her to do it. Overly strict parents don't help their children develop an "internal" locus of decision making.)

10. The world is a scary place, so parents shouldn't add to it by making their kids afraid of them. Parents should avoid making any rules. (*False.* Your job is to prepare kids to live life. But because the world is a scary place, it's important that children are prepared for it every step of the way before they face adult responsibilities. Permissiveness is never a good strategy.)

Children need to understand that Mom and Dad aren't always going to be around to save them.

11. Kids are more mature these days. (*False*. They know more. They are more sophisticated and develop physically at a younger age, but that's not the same as wise maturity. Some adults want to think their children are mature because it is an excuse to back out of their parenting responsibilities, but kids are kids. Let's never forget that. Why do so many adults want to rob kids of a childhood? Kids know a lot more about a lot of things. But do they have the tools to deal with it all? The answer is usually NO.)

12. This is a new day and age. Kids don't need a dad. (*False*. Research clearly demonstrates that kids without a father struggle more than those from two-parent families. That doesn't mean they can't make it, but it is tougher for them.)

13. It's impossible for a single parent to raise a healthy child these days. (*False*. Single parents can and will continue to do a commendable job of child-rearing. The best scenario is a home with both a mom and dad who love one another. However, with the support of other adults, a single parent can provide the necessary resources spiritually, emotionally, and physically for a child to grow up healthy.)

14. There are kids who need a "tougher" kind of love. (*True*. "Tough Love" is a nationwide program that helps parents deal with children who are very strong-willed, habitually disobedient, and who don't respond well to normal disciplinary actions. These young people establish a long history of irresponsible behavior. Parents are urged to take a very strong stand against tremendously immature and destructive behavior. However, make sure you aren't trying to apply tough love techniques to a situation that doesn't need it or you could worsen the situation.)

15. It's okay to rescue children from their own mistakes. (*False*. Too many parents spend too much time trying to "rescue" their children from natural and logical consequences of their behavior. Children need to understand that Mom and Dad aren't always going to be around to save them. This is a scary world. Kids who are looking to someone else to face it for them won't develop the life skills necessary to deal with the wide variety of experiences and choices ahead of them.)

Conclude the session by having the participants team up with partners where they will each identify one of the "parenting issues" that they find most challenging and share why. Then they can pray for each other.

WE Can Help Our Kids Do It!

10

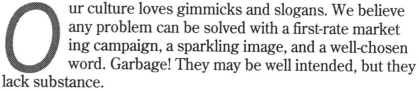

Session Aim:
To help parents teach their children how to evaluate and make wise, godly choices, which will keep them from destructive paths.

Our culture loves gimmicks and slogans. We believe any problem can be solved with a first-rate marketing campaign, a sparkling image, and a well-chosen word. Garbage! They may be well intended, but they lack substance.

Do you believe guns will disappear from the street if we offer a "guns for sneakers" program? Do you believe that "Just say No!" to drugs really works? It may have some value in deglamorizing drugs, but life is too complex for it to have much impact on users.

It is good to hear anti-violence raps and star basketball players encourage our kids to "Work hard, don't be afraid to sweat for what you want, you can do it if you choose to do it." But positive media campaigns are useful only if they are part of a larger strategy . . . the strategy of the home.

Parents can teach their children to think about the consequences of their actions before a mistake is made. They are able to give guidelines to assist their children in understanding how to make wise choices. Parents can also help form their children's conscience.

If we need a slogan, let it be, "Parents, WE can help our kids do it!"

Parents can teach their children to think about the consequences of their actions before a mistake is made.

Getting Ready

Scriptures:
Matthew 7:13, 14;
Romans 1:20.

1. Photocopy enough copies of "Consequences" (RS-10A) and "What I Want to Build into My Child" (RS-10B).
2. Prepare large sheets of newsprint or butcher paper to cover table tops. (The number of tables depends on the size of your group. Make sure everyone can fit around a table. If tables are not available, people can work on the floor, or the sheets can be taped to the wall.) Bring a sufficient number crayons or colored markers for everyone to use. Ahead of time draw a path (starting at one end of the paper) that quickly divides into a straight narrow path and a broad winding path. This is for use in Step 2.

❶ Just Say "No!"

Objective:
To examine the ineffectiveness of popular slogans to help kids avoid trouble (5-10 minutes).

Ask participants these questions, soliciting their responses by a show of hands.

- **How many of you want your child to resist negative peer pressure?**
- **How many of you want your child to avoid gang involvement?**
- **How many of you don't want your child to be a victim of violence?**
- **How many of you don't want your child carrying a gun?**
- **How many of you don't want your child fighting?**
- **How many of you don't want your child watching violent movies?**
- **How many of you don't want your children following the advice of the "gangsta" rappers or heavy-metal performers?**

Look the parents in the eye and tell them, **All you have to do to keep your children from these things is to tell them one thing, and everything will be okay. Ready? The magic formula . . . tell your children to "Just say No!" That's all you have to do.**

Pause for about a minute as you look from one person to the other. (It will seem like an eternity, but stretch it out as long as you can.)

Since the early '80s we have been teaching kids to say "no!" Has it been effective? The statistics report that sexually transmitted diseases,[1] teen pregnancy, and violent crimes have all increased dramatically.[2] Drug

Drug use appears to be dropping among younger African-American, urban children . . . due to its bitter consequences. . . ."

usage is also terribly high and still rising among most teenagers. (Ironically, *Newsweek* magazine recently reported that drug use appears to be dropping among younger African-American, urban children—not because of slogans or anti-drug programs, but due to its bitter consequences in their own homes and neighborhoods.[3])

What are some of the good things the slogan campaigns have done? (The campaigns get the majority of the public to become aware of the problem. They help younger kids become aware and exposed to warnings at an early age. It's good to see positive comments in the media.)

What is ineffective about these positive slogan campaigns? (A person may give lip service to something that does not come from the heart. When a person says "no," he or she could mean "maybe," or "talk to me a little more about what you have in mind and I might say " 'yes.' " These kind of campaigns usually don't work with older children. Saying, "Just say no" to anyone who's already addicted is "just plain silly.")

Make two columns on the board. Label one column **NO**; the other **YES**. Record the group's responses to the following questions in the appropriate column.

What do you want your children to say "no" to? Think about the lessons we have already covered and include those ideas. (We want our children to say "no" to garbage in media, violent activity, premarital sex, materialism, secularism, gangs, drugs, etc.)

What are some of the negative consequences of saying, "no"? (Peer problems, loneliness, getting beat up for convictions, ridicule, etc.)

What do you want your children to say "yes" to? (Healthy recreational programs, family relationships, good music and entertainment, family, school, Jesus Christ, positive peer pressure, etc.).

Are there any consequences to this behavior? (Feeling good about one's self. Others may want to follow you. Eternal life.)

Leave these responses on the board.

❷ Finding the Narrow Path

Objective:

To help parents inform their children what the narrow path is and how to get on it (15 minutes).

Have everyone turn to Matthew 7:13, 14 as you read the verse aloud: **"Enter through the narrow gate. For wide is the gate and broad is the road that leads to destruction, and many enter through it. But small is the gate and narrow the road that leads to life, and only a few find it."**

Is the NO column the wide or narrow road? (Obviously, it is the wider road.)

Invite the group members to gather around the large sheets of newsprint (on tables, floor, or walls). Provide crayons or colored markers. Have people within each group number off as "1" or "2." Ask all the "1s" to draw something along the narrow path that they would like their kids to say "yes" to. Have all the "2s" draw something along the broad path that might entice a young person to take that way. Warn the groups that they have only five minutes for their creation.

When the time is up, encourage everyone to note what others have drawn. Some explanation may be in order.

Why are so many people choosing the broad path? (There is a lot of company on this way. It's the popular way. While the things on this path aren't good for you, they provide short-term pleasure.)

Why does the narrow path have only a few people on it? (To follow this road, one must make a choice. Because it is narrow, it is easier to get off the path, therefore it requires a real commitment. It's a lonelier road. Even before you get on it, this road looks harder and less fun.)

As Christian parents we want our kids on the narrow road. Our desire is for our children to experience "life" as God defines it. Slogans and gimmicks aren't enough to keep someone walking along the narrow path.

How would you describe a "narrow path" lifestyle? (It's a pattern of life in which we choose godly behavior. It's having sufficient faith to keep our eyes focused on Jesus.) **What skills are necessary to make "narrow path" lifestyle decisions?** (A good conscience. Courage to follow through on decisions. Sufficient information to make good decisions. Being able to think beforehand and evaluate the consequences of one's behavior.)

Our kids need to learn to say "no!" and they need to understand the rewards of saying "yes!" However, they also need to know why they are making those decisions and to have the skills necessary to choose the better

way. To live this kind of life, our youth must have faith that will take them through some hard times. Courage is essential to continue walking along the path when others are not. Our kids need to know that saying "no" is just one strategy for a narrow-road lifestyle.

❸ Teaching "Narrow-Path" Living

Objective:
To help parents understand that "narrow-path" living is a long process and requires consistent modeling (10 minutes).

Parents cannot be involved intimately with every detail of their children's lives. However, as William Kilpatrick writes in *Why Johnny Can't Tell Right from Wrong* . . .

> Parents need to be working toward the creation of what Louis Sullivan, the secretary of health and human services, calls a "Culture of Character." As Sullivan says, "A new culture of character in America nurtured by strengthened families and communities, would do much to alleviate the alienation, isolation and despair that fuel teen pregnancy, violence, drug and alcohol abuse and other social problems afflicting us. . . . Study after study has shown that children who are raised in an environment of strong values tend to thrive in every sense.[4]

Explore with the parents how one goes about creating a "Culture of Character" that can be the launching pad for a "narrow-road" lifestyle. To stimulate discussion, ask how successful the following approaches are:

- **Wishing it will happen.**
- **Hoping it will happen.**
- **Expecting others to do it for you.**
- **Forcing it into your children.**
- **Yelling it into your children.**
- **Letting kids figure it out for themselves.**

Since these methods don't work—never have, never will—ask group members what will work.

There's an old maxim that says: "Give a man a fish and you'll feed him for a day. Teach him to fish and he'll eat for a lifetime." Longshoreman and philosopher Eric Hoffer once said, "In times of change, learners inherit the earth, while the learned find themselves beautifully equipped to deal with a world that no longer exists."

Ask the group to discuss the advantages of teaching our children "how to fish" and encouraging them to become learners. List their responses on the board. (This method has long-term benefits. We will not always be with our children, so it's wise to teach them certain things now. Children need to learn how to handle situations in life. Children can become independent of us.)

What does teaching our children to fish and encouraging them to become learners mean in terms of parental commitment? (We have to be committed to teaching the principles, allowing experiences so they can learn, letting go, and taking risks.)

What keeps parents away from this kind of an approach? (It's time consuming. It takes a commitment. It can feel risky. We may not know how to do it.)

Now, ask parents to think back to the time when they learned to ride a bike. Ask them to describe elements of that learning experience. Write them on the board. This list should include things like:

(• There was someone there to help me.
• I made a lot of mistakes.
• I learned from my mistakes.
• I tried different techniques until I found one that worked.
• It was hard.
• I got hurt.
• Once I learned, I never forgot.
• I almost did it, but then I fell.
• Wobbly was good enough at first.
• I gained confidence to try without help.)

How is learning to ride a bike similar to teaching our children how to choose a "narrow-road" lifestyle and saying "no" to negative pressures? (The responses should be similar to our learning to ride a bike experience noted above.)

Teaching our children to walk the narrow path is the same way. We can't just hope they'll do it. We can't expect them to know how. Walking through the mine-

field of our culture and choosing the narrow way will require:

- A mentor (preferably Mom or Dad).
- Willingness to take risks to learn how to make decisions.
- A lot of mistakes and learning from those mistakes.
- Uncertainty tempered with faith.
- Hurt.
- Prayer.
- A firm hand.
- Someone to be there when you fall.
- A ton of encouragement.

❹ "Narrow-Path" Living and Consequences

Objective:
To think through the value of establishing consequences for our children's actions (10 minutes).

Write the word CONSEQUENCES on the board. Explain to the group that an important aspect of teaching our kids to walk the narrow path includes not rescuing them from the consequences of their actions unless those consequences are so dire that we would be acting irresponsibly.

Under the word CONSEQUENCES write on the left NATURAL and on the right LOGICAL. **What are the natural results of an action?** (The consequences that arise from the behavior. For instance, if you turn the wrong way when riding a bicycle, you may lose your balance, fall off, and hurt yourself. When you forget your lunch at home, you go hungry during the lunch hour. When you don't study for a test, you risk failure.)

What are logical consequences? (They are results that need to be imposed when the natural consequences aren't obvious.)

Under LOGICAL write the words Related, Respectful, Revealed, Reasonable. **According to Jane Nelsen in her book *Positive Discipline*,[5] a good logical consequence is related to the incident, it respects the child, if at all possible it is revealed ahead of time (negotiated with child), and it is reasonable (teaches rather than punishes).**

For example, if a child is involved in a fight with another child, he or she will suffer whatever the results of fighting might be (natural consequence). But in addi-

tion, he or she has to pay for the ripped jacket of the other person (logical consequence).

What do you think will happen to children who are not raised in a consequential environment? (They will think they are able to do anything and never have to suffer for it. They think parents or someone will always bail them out, and they will never learn responsibility for their own actions.)

What will happen to children who find themselves in an environment where parents want to use consequences to punish rather than teach? (The children will experience anger, frustration, rebellion, etc. There will be frequent negative confrontations, etc.)

Give each person the handout entitled, "Consequences" (RS-11A). Encourage them to study it at home as a further resource for understanding how various consequences relate to parenting.

❺ Knowing Right from Wrong

Objective:
To explore ways of nurturing the conscience of young people (5-15 minutes).

Charles Colson paid a stiff penalty for his choices. He was a major player in the Nixon White House scandal, commonly known as "Watergate." At the time, he felt he was above the law. As a result, he went to prison. Now, he heads a ministry to prison inmates. At the dedication of the Focus on the Family building in Colorado Springs, Colson made these remarks about conscience.

We are witnessing in America the most terrifying thing that could happen to a society—the death of conscience. . . . Where does conscience come from? It is something God gave us at birth, but it has to be cultivated. . . .

Aristotle said virtue consists of not merely *knowing* what is right, but also in having the will *to do* what is right, and the will is trained by practice, by choosing to do right continually until it becomes a habit. . . .

That is why what is happening to the family today is so dangerous. Adults are spending 40 percent less time with their kids than their parents spent with them. . . .

Because these parents are not cultivating conscience in their children we are producing a generation of 12 year olds who are roaming the streets with pistols, shooting one another.

The second way in which conscience is cultivated is through moral consensus—the values and moral truth a society shares and the rules people agree to live by. . . .

Presently, our society is walking down a dangerous path where there are no moral values, no absolute truth that tells us how we should live.[6]

Ask for a show of hands on how many believe violence is a result of people who never learned right from wrong and how many believe it is a result of people who know the difference, but choose to ignore what is right.

This is an interesting, ongoing debate. We know that too many young people haven't had the love, care, and nurture necessary to fully cultivate their sense of right and wrong. Their consciences are undeveloped and sputtering along. However, that's not the last word on the issue.

Have someone read Romans 1:20, then comment: **So even with a conscience that hasn't been cultivated, there is no excuse for sin. We may find some explanations, but there are no excuses.**

Ask the participants to form a "pinwheel" by dividing the group into two equal parts. Have one part form a circle with their chairs facing outward (**O**). Have the other group form a circle around the first circle with their chairs facing inward (**X**). They should be opposite someone from the other group. For each question you read, the participants in the outer circle will move one chair to the right in order to face a new partner. They can discuss a question until you call time and read a new question. Keep this moving quickly.

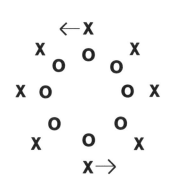

- **Is Colson right? Are there too many young people running around without a good sense of right and wrong?**
- **Do you think the violence in today's culture is a result of people who never learned right from wrong or because they chose to ignore what's right?**
- **Who helped you form your conscience?**
- **What did that person(s) do to cultivate your conscience?**

Get parents thinking about their goals for their children. . . .

- **What are some of the things that are wrong in our culture that you want your children to know about?**
- **How will you teach your children that in a violent world there can be some very disastrous consequences to actions?**
- **What role does faith play in the development of conscience?**

Before closing the session in prayer, ask the parents to prepare for the next session by completing "What I Want to Build into My Child" (RS-10B). Emphasize the importance of their finishing it before the nest session and bringing it back next time. If there is time, allow them to begin it before closing. The purpose of the activity is to get parents thinking about their goals for their children and how they want to go about building certain qualities, beliefs, values, perceptions, and skills into their children's lives.

Close in prayer by asking God to help each parent find time to prayerfully consider how to apply the materials in this session. Also thank Him for parents who want to make a positive difference in their children's lives.

Notes:

1. "Adolescence, 13-18," *Free to Be Family* (Washington, D.C.: Family Research Council, 1992), 77, 78.

2. William J. Bennett, *The Index of Leading Cultural Indicators* (New York: Simon and Schuster, 1994), 22, 23, 30, 31, 74, 75.

3. Carroll Bogert, "Good News on Drugs from the Inner City," *Newsweek*, February 14, 1994, 28, 29.

4. William Kilpatrick, *Why Johnny Can't Tell Right From Wrong; Moral Literacy and the Case for Character Education* (New York: Simon and Schuster, 1992), 252.

5. Jane Nelsen, *Positive Discipline* (New York: Ballantine, 1987).

6. Chuck Colson, "Where Did Our Conscience Go?" *Focus on the Family* magazine, January 1994, 12, 13.

The Devil Made Me Do It!

11

Session Aim:
To help parents see the need for a strong sense of right and wrong and equip them to assist their children in developing one.

Remember the cartoon, "Tweety Bird and Sylvester"? The little old lady goes out, leaving behind her cherished pets, Sylvester the Cat and Tweety Bird, a canary. Sylvester is usually napping on the floor while Tweety Bird is singing in a cage.

At first all seems well. Then a miniature devil hops onto Sylvester's shoulder. It is dressed in red, with a pitchfork, long tail and horns. "Sylvester," the voice allures, "wouldn't you like to have Tweety Bird for lunch?" Before you know it, Sylvester is licking his chops.

Then another image hops onto Sylvester's other shoulder. This one is dressed like an angel, decked out in a white robe, with a halo and harp. "Now, Sylvester," the angel encourages, "you don't want to eat your friend Tweety Bird. How disappointed Granny would be to come home and find her Tweety Bird eaten by the cat."

In every episode, Sylvester ignores the angel and attempts to capture Tweety Bird. The bird always escapes in the nick of time while Sylvester ends up beaten, bitten, or badly wounded.

A profound message in a cartoon. God's way is always best. Satan's way always leads to destruction. This session will help parents convey this lesson to their children. We always have a choice. And in our day full of violence and anger, the wrong choice could mean death.

God's way is always best. Satan's way always leads to destruction.

Getting Ready:

Scriptures:
Luke 14:25-34.

1. Photocopy "What I Want to Build into My Child" (RS-10B) from last week for anyone who might have forgotten theirs.
2. Photocopy "Parenting Strategies" (RS-11A) and "A Dialogue . . . Good Parenting at Work" (RS-11B) for everyone. Make an extra copy of RS-11A . Both resources are two pages.
3. Cut up the extra copy of RS-11A for use in Step 4 (see page 83).
4. Before the session contact two parents and ask them to do a skit based on "A Dialogue . . . Good Parenting at Work" (RS-11B). Get copies of the skit to the "actors" before the session if possible. If they can't get together to rehearse the skit on their own, suggest that they come a half hour early to practice. They do not need to memorize their parts, just be familiar enough with them to read convincingly.
5. Write these questions on the board ahead of time for use in Step 2:
   • Is what you want to build into your child based upon principles from God's Word? Upon which ones?
   • When you think of the parenting task before you, how do you feel?
   • What do you need to start doing today to accomplish what you are setting out to do?
   • How can the Body of Christ help?

❶ Rethinking Some of the Old Advice

Objectives:
To help parents reconsider some traditional parental advice that may be harmful to their children (10 minutes).

After reading each of the following bits of advice, allow the group time for discussion.

These following comments may have been okay for parents to say to their children twenty years ago, but how could they cause problems today?

1. "If somebody hits you, hit them back." (This may cost you your life. It may be better to walk away or report the incident to the teacher. Fist fights are almost a thing of the past. The other person might pull a gun or knife from his or her pocket.)

2. "If the bully and his buddies mess with you, beat up the bully, and his buddies will leave you alone." (A bully and his buddies today are probably gangbangers. They may be trying to get you into their gang. Beating up the leader may cause more problems, and once again, cost you your life. If at all possible, walk away.)

3. You see a nice jacket on sale for your son. You bring it home, and he has a funny expression on his face. But you say, "Like it or not, it's a fine jacket and you're gonna wear it. I don't want to hear anything else about it." (The jacket may be something gang members wear or the colors of a gang. Listen to your child when they prefer not to wear a certain color or item. Also be attentive if your child wants to wear a certain color all the time. It may indicate he or she is trying to associate with a gang.)

4. "You want me to take you to school and pick you up? What's the matter with you? You think you're too good to ride the bus?" (Your child may be legitimately afraid or trying to avoid trouble with someone at school or on the bus. Listen and look into what your child is saying. Make sure that's not the reason before forcing him or her to go someplace.)

5. "Don't go running to the teacher every time someone messes with you. They will label you a snitch." (Allowing a teacher or security guard to handle a problem is wiser than trying to deal with it yourself. Religious youth, nerds, straight kids, and snitches usually don't get harassed by gang members. They are too much of a risk. Bearing the ridicule of an unflattering label may be a matter of survival.)

Encourage parents to teach their kids that reporting a crime is not being a snitch.

If you have only forty-five minutes for your session, skip to Step 3.

❷ What Will My Child Say about Me When I'm Ninety?

Objective:
To help parents begin to set goals for each child (10 minutes).

Break the group into small teams of three or four people each and have them read aloud their speeches from the back of their resource sheet, "What I Want to Build into My Child " (RS-10B) that was assigned as preparation for this session. For those who may not have prepared, encourage them to share what they would like one of their children to say about them at their ninetieth birthday party.

When the team members have given their speeches, tell them to discuss with each other their plans for building specific things into the lives of their children.

For the sake of your child, you have to do things that you otherwise would not want to do.

After the parents have finished discussing the questions on RS-10B, have them answer the questions you wrote on the board ahead of time. Allow a few volunteers to share their answers. Ask: **In what ways can we as concerned parents help each other?**

❸ We've Come This Far by Faith

Objective:
To discover the parallels between Jesus' comments about the cost of being a disciple with the challenges of being a good parent (10 minutes).

With the parents still in their separate teams (divide the group into teams of three or four each if you have not already done so), ask them to open their Bibles to Luke 14:25-34. Have everyone read it silently. Give each team an assignment based on the passage. If you have more than four teams, duplicate assignments as needed.

Team 1: How is being a parent like "carrying the cross" and being Jesus' disciple? (For the sake of your child, you have to do things that you otherwise would not want to do. It is a heavy responsibility.)

Team 2: How was doing the take-home assignment like "building the tower"? (It's part of the process of counting the cost of raising a godly child. You have to add up the expense, it will cost you something. You need a firm foundation.)

Team 3: How was doing the take-home assignment like a king preparing for war? (We are preparing our kids for spiritual battle. We need a strategy and a plan and we need to gather the resources to accomplish the task.)

Team 4: How is a parent to avoid losing his or her saltiness? (By following God, staying on top of things, working hard, etc. Salt preserves food from decay, and we must resist corruption in our own lives and in the lives of our families.)

Reunite the whole group and have each team share the best of their findings.

**cknowledge that each child is unique and parents must be sensitive to the differences.**

❹ With God's Help, You Can Do It

Objective:
To show parents how they can start building into the lives of their children necessary perceptions and skills (10 minutes).

Before the group time, you should have cut apart a copy of "Parenting Strategies" (RS-11A). Divide up the slips of strategies so that each class member gets about the same number, excluding the two people who will be doing the skit. Point out that the numbers on the slips are for reference later and do not indicate the order used in the skit.

Explain that in a few minutes there will be a skit (see RS-11B) and that during it you want the class members to watch for the particular strategies they have been given. At the end of the dramatization they will share how they saw their strategies portrayed in the skit.

Explain that this dramatization is designed to share some realistic, doable, and necessary parenting strategies that will help equip their sons and daughters for living in a violent culture.

The script for the skit is "A Dialogue . . . Good Parenting at Work" (RS-11B). The "actors" should have rehearsed ahead of time. Ask them to perform it at this point.

❺ Learning from Others

Objective:
To identify skills and attitudes for parents to use with their children (10-15 minutes).

Pass out additional complete copies of "Parenting Strategies" (RS-11A) as a reference for all parents. Have them share where they saw "their strategies" (the slips in their hands) at work.

Generate discussion by asking questions such as:

How could using these strategies in our homes help us in equipping our children to live in a violent world?

Do any of these strategies appear more necessary than others?

How might both the child and the parent feel after an interaction like this?

Have group members share about their successes with using these or similar strategies. Ask what other strategies they might use.

Some of the parents might suggest that the skit looks good on paper, but is unrealistic in the real world of their home. It's possible that some parents believe in a very strict, punitive approach to parenting. Do not get in a debate with them, but ask how the parenting strategy they are using is working and how their child is responding. Ask if they feel comfortable that it is preparing their child adequately to make his or her own decisions. Don't put the parents on the spot, just encourage thoughtful evaluation.

Or some parents may be dealing with severe problems that need professional intervention. If this is the case, you may want to suggest some qualified Christian counselors in your community. Don't try to turn the session into a therapy time.

Acknowledge that each child is unique and parents must be sensitive to the differences. These basic strategies can be effectively used with all children.

❻ Planning Your Personal Strategy

Objective:
To enable parents to identify the strategies they need to add to their toolbox of parenting skills (5 minutes).

Ask parents to quickly review the list of strategies. Have them circle the numbers of two or three ideas that they want to personally develop.

Conclude by referring back to Luke 14:25-34 in terms of helping the parents retain their "saltiness." If your group is small enough for everyone to pray, keep the whole group together. Otherwise, divide into smaller groups.

Either in one large group or a few smaller groups, have parents stand and hold hands. Invite them to complete this statement with the strategy they would like to make more a part of their parenting toolbox : **The parenting strategy that might help me keep my saltiness is_____ . Lord help me do this.**

Building on a Firm
12 Foundation

Session Aim:
To provide practical parenting techniques and strategies for helping at-risk youth cope in a violent, aggressive society.

1. A commitment and love for Jesus Christ, our Lord and Savior.

2. An understanding of the benefits believers have in Jesus Christ.

3. A knowledge and understanding of my ethnic history, starting with the Bible.

4. A strong work ethic.

5. An understanding and desire for the God-instituted family.

6. Respect for authority.

7. An appreciation for knowledge, education, and wisdom.

8. Self-dignity, self-control, and self-respect.

9. Respect for others.

10. A basic understanding of financial systems.

Help parents see the need for developing the character of their children.

Getting Ready

Scriptures:
John 14:1, 6; Ephesians 1:3, 8, 13; Exodus 13:8, 9; Genesis 1:28; 2:15, 23-25; Romans 13:1; Proverbs 1:7-9; 30:8, 9; Titus 2:11-13; Matthew 22:39.

1. Prepare enough copies for everyone of "A Firm Foundation" (RS-12A), "Character Quality Checklist" (RS-12B), and "The Church and the Development of Youth" (RS-12C).
2. On the top of ten different blank sheets of paper write one character quality (listed on pages 85 and 87 and RS-12A), and leave the rest of the page blank.
3. On the board RANDOMLY list the Scripture references in the right-hand column on page 87 for use in Step 2.

❶ Why African-American Youth Need These Character Qualities

Objective:
To help parents see the need for developing the character of their children (10-15 minutes).

Pass out copies of "A Firm Foundation" (RS-12A). Assign each individual or couple (depending on the size of your group) one of the ten qualities. Ask them to act out a commercial, selling that character quality. The buyers are parents, but the products should be geared toward young people.

Encourage their imaginations, and have fun with this exercise. For example, one might say, "Here's a bottle of Jesus Christ, drink it and you'll get your values in order. If you have a teenager at home this is just the thing to get him or her through those challenging years."

After each commercial presentation have the participants write down in the center column on their "A Firm Foundation" resource sheet (RS-12A) two or three reasons why this quality is needed.

❷ What the Bible Has to Say about Character

Objectives:
To look examples of character qualities from God's Word (10 minutes).

Either read or have a volunteer read aloud the Scripture passages you have RANDOMLY listed on the board ahead of time. Have group members try to match each Scripture with the right character quality. Encourage group interaction in establishing the match. When the correct match has been made, ask the participants to write in the reference and add a few summary words in the box on the right side of the chart on RS-12A.

The filled-in chart on "A Firm Foundation" (RS-12A) might look something like the chart on the following page.

All children need a commitment and love for Jesus Christ, our Lord and Savior.

Character Quality	Reasons It Is Needed	Biblical Basis
1. A commitment and love for Jesus Christ, our Lord and Savior.	• Salvation. • Full, satisfying life. • Guidance, purpose, and meaning in life.	John 14:1, 6—Jesus is the only way to God and truth.
2. An understanding of the benefits believers have in Jesus Christ.	• Know what's available to us in this life. • We will grow and mature as Christians. • More joy, peace, and satisfaction in life.	Eph. 1:3, 7, 8, 13 3—All blessings 7—Forgiveness 8—All wisdom 13—Holy Spirit
3. A knowledge and understanding of ethnic history, starting with the Bible.	• To know where we have come from and where we are going. • To build appropriate pride and self-esteem in ourselves and our race.	Exod. 13:8, 9—God wanted Israel to know and preserve history.
4. A strong work ethic.	• God invented it. • Good for you. • Helps keep you out of poverty, crime, and debt.	Gen. 2:15—God put people to work in the garden.
5. An understanding and desire for the God-instituted family.	• God instituted it. • God wants to use it. • It is a picture of Christ and the church.	Gen. 1:28; 2:23-25—God put man and woman together, then, told them to multiply.
6. Respect for authority.	• God placed us all under authority. • Helps us learn to submit to Him.	Rom. 13:1—God's order.
7. An appreciation for knowledge, education, and wisdom.	• Helps obtain employment. • To know how to do things. • To know what God wants us to do.	Prov. 1:7-9—Desire these qualities.
8. Self-dignity, self-control, and self-respect.	• Respect self. • Complete tasks.	Titus 2:11-13—God wants us to be self-controlled. Matt. 22:39—Love ourselves.
9. A respect for others.	• Keep us from being self-absorbed. • Reflect God and show His power.	Matt. 22:39—Love your neighbor.
10. A basic understanding of financial systems.	• To survive. • To not be in poverty. • To help each other.	Prov. 30:8, 9—Desire neither poverty nor riches but just what is needed.

❸ How Firm Is Your Foundation?

Objective:
To have parents brainstorm and share ways to build specific character qualities in their children (15-20 minutes).

Ask participants to choose one character quality (besides a commitment to Christ) and share how God has developed it in their lives. Try to get at least one comment on each quality.

Distribute the sheets you prepared ahead of time with a character quality written at the top of each one. Have the parents write suggested ways to develop this quality in their children. If your group is large, divide into smaller groups. Have people switch papers every few minutes so that several people give input on each quality. As a group, discuss the suggestions listed.

Virtually all parents and kids are aware of many great Caucasian Americans such as George Washington, Abraham Lincoln, etc. They may not be as aware of the contributions of great Americans of other ethnic heritages. To emphasize the importance of building strong character, share as many of the following sketches of great Americans as your time will allow.

- **Early in life, Dr. E.V. Hill understood God's power and the gifts He gave to him. His faith in God moved him from the cotton fields in the South to a position as one of the most dynamic African-American pastors, speakers, and leaders in the country.**

- **Mary McLeod Bethune, a graduate of Moody Bible Institute in Chicago, loved learning and desired to see other minorities educated. In 1904 she founded a school for girls. It later merged with Cookman Institute to become Bethune-Cookman College.**

- **Athletes provide many examples of self-discipline and strong character. In 1988 Florence Griffith Joyner won three gold and two silver Olympic medals in the area of track and field. Kristi Yamaguchi, women's figure skating 1992 Olympic Gold Medalist, inspires Asian-American and all youth. Michael Chang, a dynamic Christian, is among the top tennis players worldwide and youngest winner of the French Open (1989).**

- **John Perkins's understanding of the importance of the family motivated him to serve as a role model for many inner-city children. He also started the Foundation for Reconciliation and Development, one of the largest African-American ministries in the country addressing several social problems.**

- **Benjamin O. Davis, Sr., was the first African American to be promoted (in 1940) to Brigadier General in the U.S. Army. Interestingly enough, his son, Benjamin O. Davis, Jr., was the first black to rise to Brigadier General in the U.S. Air Force (in 1954). He went on to become a Lieutenant General.**

- **Malcolm X and Rev. Martin Luther King, Jr., were men of self-discipline, dignity, and respect. They refused to allow society to continue to unfairly treat and put down the black race. They made major strides for the civil rights cause.**

- **Korean Pastor Paul Y. Cho recognized the importance of spiritual discipline and prayer. As head pastor of the largest church in the world, he has developed principles of personal and corporate spiritual growth which benefit believers worldwide.**

- **Sojourner Truth's commitment to her fellow human beings caused her to risk her life several times to bring slaves north to freedom.**

If we develop these characteristics in our youth, they can have a widespread impact for good.

Pass out the "Character Qualities Checklist and Goals" (RS-12B) so participants can think through how they are doing in developing character in their children's lives. After they have finished the checklist, challenge them to take the goal sheet home and fill it out and begin to work on some of the areas mentioned.

❹ The Church and the Youth in Your Community

Objective:
To examine ways the church has been, and can continue to be, a vital part of the development of youth (15-20 minutes).

Pass out copies of "The Church and the Development of Youth" (RS-12C). Divide the group into three or four small teams. Assign each team this challenge: **Your pastor has asked you to be youth director for your church. You have an unlimited budget, staff, resources, etc. Develop a brief youth development program, using the suggestions from the work sheet and the qualities talked about earlier.**

Have the group come back together and share their ideas.

Conclude the session with prayer for at-risk youth and the ideas presented.

Where Do We Go from Here?

13

Session Aim:
To provide parents practical suggestions for helping their children avoid violence and become street smart and to be catalysts for developing a healthier community.

I knew Tyrone depended on the school to supply clean clothes and food. But I never realized how much school meant to this little seven-year-old until I arrived one morning to find him outside the front doors, cradling his left arm, his brown eyes wet with held-back tears.

His arm looked horrible. It hurt just to look at the raw third-degree burns exposed to the cold morning air. I could only imagine Tyrone's pain. . . .

He explained that he had been helping his mother pour hot grease from a frying pan into a glass jar to store for the next use. He was steadying the jar when it burst, spilling the scalding oil onto his arm.

There was no phone in the house to call for help. There was no transportation to the hospital. But there was the school. Tyrone knew when he went to bed that night, biting his lip to endure the pain, that morning would come and with it would come his teachers, his principal, and the open doors of that building and with them would come help.

—*Madeline Cartwright in* For the Children[1]

We need more safe places for the thousands of little Tyrones in our communities.

In our violent world, our kids need to know where to go and where not to go.

Getting Ready

Scriptures:

Proverbs 1:10-19 (Living Bible); Romans 12:9-21.

1. Provide large poster boards or newsprint for the map exercise in Step 1. You will need one board for each team of three people.
2. Provide enough marking pens so that each team of three people can have a black marker, plus a red, blue, and green marking pen (substitute other colors if necessary).
3. Photocopy "Keeping Our Kids Out of Trouble" (RS-13A), "When Your Child Has Witnessed Violence" (RS-13B), and " 'Deliver Us from Evil' " (RS-13C) for everyone.
4. If possible, provide a cassette recorder and tape to play some soft instrumental music during the reflection time in Step 5.

❶ To Be Forewarned Is to Be Forearmed

Objective:

To identify places in the community that children should avoid, go to for help, and become involved in positive activities (10 minutes).

As you begin this session, divide the group into teams of three and provide each team with a poster board, a black marker, and three different colored markers (e.g., red, blue, and green).

In our violent world, our kids need to know where to go and where not to go. They need to know what to do if they are faced with violence or the threat of it. In this exercise, we'll try and provide some guidelines.

Have the small groups draw maps of your community. They don't have to be to scale or very pretty, but they should have a few of the basic landmarks: major streets, parks, notable buildings, or stores, etc.

On their maps, instruct the parents to indicate with a red marker places of potential violence. This could mean homes where parents allow children to do anything they want, areas with a high-crime profile, loitering sites for gangbangers, or drug houses.

Indicate with a blue marker places the children could go for help. Identify the fire stations, police stations, and youth centers they should know about.

Indicate with a green marker places where the children could get involved with positive activities. These might include: a church with a good youth program, parachurch organizations, drop-in centers, Y's, supervised gyms, Little League, soccer programs, homes of families with shared values, etc.

Have the teams share their maps with the whole group.

Encourage the parents to repeat this activity with their children, providing a chance to talk with their children about

why some places are safe while others are not. The children might know of dangerous places and positive resources that their parents are not aware of.

Option: If the kids of the parents in your group are highly mobile (beyond a defined neighborhood), distribute copies of a regional map of your area to each small group. Using the designated colored markers, have the parents put numbers on the maps to identify places of violence, help, and positive activities, as described above. Then on an accompanying sheet of newsprint, have them duplicate the colored numbers listing the corresponding locations. For instance, "fire station" might be written next to the blue number 2, "supervised gym" next to the green number 4, etc.

❷ Street Smarts Versus Fear

Objective:
To identify street-smart wisdom that our children need to possess (10-15 minutes).

Do we want to teach our children to fear the world they live in? No. However, they need to respect what is happening in the world and understand the consequences. Children should have a healthy understanding of the world they live in and not be uninformed or naive. A lack of knowledge in a violent culture could lead to serious injury, even death. They should be able to pick up clues or signals that indicate possible dangerous situations. It is good to be able to think safely and heed warnings. Youth need to be equipped with decision-making skills to stay out of trouble.

Our kids need to be street smart and know what to look for and what to do if they see trouble coming their way. Remember the activity in Session 5 when we drew pictures of a culturally relevant, media-oriented child? Let's do the same thing. But this time draw a picture of the street-smart kid.

What does he or she need to have in order to make it in the world? (Possibly big eyes, in order to clearly see what is happening in the particular surroundings. Quick feet in order to run, if they see trouble coming their way. A razor-sharp mind for making quick decisions. Open, nonthreatening hands, and a closed mouth.)

This time do the exercise in the large group. Ask someone who is a good artist to draw the picture on the board. Use the drawing as a catalyst for talking about street smarts.

Ask: **Are street smarts the same as common sense?**

Anyone who has been labeled as a troublemaker needs to know how to handle the possibility of police harrassment.

(Unfortunately, common sense doesn't take you as far as you need to go in uncommon situations.)

Draw out of the group what they feel are essential "street smarts" needed for your particular community. Ask the group members to raise their hands if they have been involved or know someone who has been a victim of police harassment or brutality. Ask one or two people to share their experience.

Unfortunately, many African-American, Latino, and Hispanic young males and anyone who has been labeled as a troublemaker can be the target of police harassment and brutality. They need to be taught how to handle these situations to avoid personal injury and unnecessary criminal charges. Pass out "Keeping Our Kids Out of Trouble" (RS-13A). Go around the room having the participants take turns reading the suggestions on the sheet. If you have time, after suggestion 8 is read, you might add the following comment by Gordon McLean, the director of the juvenile justice ministry of Metro Chicago Youth for Christ:

> **The police don't like this card. But the reason we encourage its use is because a young person can often be lured or trapped into making an incriminating statement. The police are interested in apprehending a suspect and clearing a case off their books. This does not always coincide with the rights of the young person . . . or even the truth. So we say there is plenty of time to talk to the police after you have consulted with your lawyer. He or she can then advise you what—if anything—is best to say. After all, in our system of justice, it is not our obligation to incriminate ourselves. If we say anything, we have to tell the truth, but we don't have to say anything.[2]**

After all the recommendations from the resource sheet have been read, ask for four volunteers to act out a skit with a police officer and a young male. Have the first pair act out the wrong way to handle a belligerent police officer. Have the other pair act out the right way. After the skits allow the group to share their reactions. Encourage parents to do this exercise at home with their children.

Pass out "When Your Child Has Witnessed Violence" (RS-13B) work sheet. If time allows, review this resource as a

*D*on't go it alone. . . . Have zero tolerance for drugs. . . . Organize neighborhood watches. . . . Refuse to live in fear.

group. If not, encourage the parents to take it home and read it. Ask everyone to keep this sheet for future reference.

❸ Taking Back the "Hood"

Objective:
To provide suggestions for how the parents can fight the negative activities in their neighborhoods (10 minutes).

Divide into two or three groups. Have each group select a spokesperson. Each group is to help prepare a one- or two-minute speech. The spokesperson has been elected president of the neighborhood block club, and the speech should include several ideas for improving the conditions on your block.

The spokespersons don't actually have to give a speech unless they want to. However, they should share their group's suggestions when the groups are back together. Write these ideas on the board. Discuss and add the following to the list if they have not been suggested.

(• Don't go it alone. Join or help create a neighborhood organization that is trying to help.

• Get to know the people on your block. Agree together to call the police at any sign of trouble.

• March. Let the gangs and criminals know this neighborhood is unified in fighting crime.

• Contact your local police. Work with them. Allow them to help you draw up a plan of action.

• Have zero tolerance for drugs. Solicit neighborhood agreement for a policy to report and insist on police response to every incidence of drug trafficking or even use. Possibly create Zero Tolerance posters for apartment entryways, store windows, and light poles.

• Organize neighborhood watches. Some neighborhoods have a car with a CB radio or cellular phone patrolling, and they alert police at any sign of trouble.

• Refuse to live in fear. If we are afraid and lock ourselves behind bars and steel doors, we have allowed the criminals to take over outside.

• Be determined. It may take time before you see anything positive happen.

• Take small steps and give it plenty of time. Most neighbor-

The problem [of drugs and gangs] can no longer be denied; the church has to become an active part of the solution.

hoods do not change overnight. You may have to try a variety of things before you find something that works in your neighborhood. Don't give up or get discouraged.)

❹ A Wake-Up Call to the Church

Objective:
To access what your church is doing to deal with the problems of violence in your neighborhood and recommend additional responses (5-10 minutes).

There are often several churches in the community, but the neighborhood is still drug and gang infested. The problem can no longer be denied; the church has to become an active part of the solution. Churches have to become involved in their community.

Discuss what your church is doing now to reduce violence in the community and what it could do to take a more active role. Here are more suggestions if the participants have not already mentioned them.

(• Pastors preach and teach God's Word and hold the members of their congregations accountable for their lifestyles.

• Realize the church is in a very strategic possession to make a change. Specifically, the black church is the only institution owned and operated by African-American people nationwide. It's the chief institution God has specifically called and blessed for the purpose of building up the black family.

• There are about three hundred thousand Christian churches and 25 million households with children in the United States. That is one church for every 83 families. We can get the job done. The church gathers weekly throughout the country. It is the only place that mobilizes large numbers of people every week in the same place.

• Contact the courts and ask about youth working community service hours at the church. Or suggest that juvenile offenders be released into the custody of men in the church instead of receiving jail sentences. The men in the church would monitor their behavior, provide employment, and help them get a new start in life.

• Develop a strong youth program. Ask questions about the church budget. How much is being spent to help the youth? Hire a full-time youth pastor.

• Invite in special speakers on marriage, parenting, gangs, violence, etc.

Conclude this series with a sense of what God is calling you to be and do.

• Provide Christian counseling for family, financial, parenting problems, etc. Develop support groups for crime victims, ex-gang members, single parents, grandparents, etc., to help them cope with difficulties.

• Provide field trips, recreational programs, and after-school program. Invite children and families in the community.

• Become active in political policies that need to be changed that affect youth, fight for better school systems, encourage parents to get on boards that make decisions concerning their youth.

• Begin a jail ministry specifically designed to evangelize local gang members. They will be out soon, and the neighborhood's only hope is if they have changed. Incarceration alone seldom makes a positive difference.)

❺ Encouragement from the Word

Objective:
To conclude this series with a sense of what God is calling you to be and do (10-15 minutes).

Romans 12:9-21 gives us some helpful insights into how we might respond to the culture of violence. Have everyone read Romans 12:9-21 silently. With soft music playing in the background, encourage the parents to reflect on the passage, asking the Lord to minister to them.

After they have finished, pass out " 'Deliver Us from Evil' " (RS-13C), and ask everyone to stand in a circle. As a responsive reading, have the parents read the bold-faced lines while you respond with the lines in normal print.

Sing "Amazing Grace" together, and close by reciting the Lord's Prayer together.

If your group would not be comfortable with singing, simply close in prayer asking God's blessing on all the children and parents or with the Lord's Prayer.

Notes:

1. Madeline Cartwright, *For the Children* (New York: Doubleday, 1993), 1, 2.
2. Gordon McLean in an interview with Dave Jackson, Feb. 24, 1994, Chicago, Ill.

Helpful Resources

Family Research Council
Fatherhood Campaign
700 13th St., N.W., Suite 500
Washington, DC 20005
(202) 783-HOME

Institute for Black Family Development
928 E. 10 Mile Road
Ferndale, MI 48220
(810) 545-7776

John M. Perkins Foundation for
Reconciliation and Development
1581 Navarro St.   or   P.O. Box 32
Pasadena, CA 91103   Jackson, MS
(818) 791-7439

Metro Chicago Youth For Christ
300 West Washington Street, Suite 416
Chicago, IL 60606
(312) 443-1YFC

Wendell Amstutz and Bart Larson
National Counseling Resource Center
P.O. Box 87
Rochester, MN 55903
(507) 281-8800

Dr. Anthony T. Evans
The Urban Alternative
P.O. Box 4000
Dallas, TX 75208
(214) 943-3868

Youth Leadership Development Programs
P.O. Box 42350
Atlanta, GA 30311
(404) 699-7606

Bibliography

Basic Parenting Resources

Arp, Dave and Claudia. *PEP Groups for PARENTS of TEENS: Building Positive Relationships for the Teen Years*. Elgin, Ill.: David C. Cook Publishing Co., 1994.

Canfield, Ken R. *The Seven Secrets of Effective Fathers*. Wheaton, Ill.: Tyndale House, 1992.

Covey, Stephen R. *The Seven Habits of Highly Effective People: Restoring the Character Ethic*. New York: Simon and Schuster, 1989.

Curran, Delores. *Traits of a Healthy Family*. San Francisco: Harper and Row, 1983.

Dobson, James. *Love Must Be Tough*. Waco, Tex.: Word Books, 1983.

_____. *Parenting Isn't for Cowards*. Waco, Tex.: Word Books, 1987.

Elkind, David. *All Grown Up and No Place to Go: Teenagers in Crisis*. Reading Mass.: Addison-Wesley Publishing Co., 1984.

Evans, Anthony. *Guiding Your Family in a Misguided World*. Colorado Springs, Colo.: Focus on the Family Publishing, 1991.

Eyre, Linda and Richard. *Teaching Your Children Values*. New York: Simon and Schuster, 1993.

Faber, Adele and Mazlish, Elaine. *How to Talk So Kids Will Listen and Listen So Kids Will Talk*. New York: Avon Books, 1980.

Glenn, H. Stephen and Nelsen, Jane. *Raising Self-Reliant Children in a Self-Indulgent World*. Rocklin, Calif.: Prima Publishing and Communications, 1989.

Huggins, Kevin. *Parenting Adolescents*. Colorado Springs, Colo.: NavPress, 1989.

Korem, Dan. *Streetwise Parents—Foolproof Kids*. Colorado Springs, Colo.: NavPress, 1992.

Leman, Kevin. *Bringing Up Kids Without Tearing Them Down*. New York: Delacorte Press, 1993.

_____. *Keeping Your Family Together When the World Is Falling Apart*. New York: Delacorte Press, 1992.

Schiller, Barbara. *Just Me & the Kids: Building Healthy Single-Parent Families*. Elgin, Ill.: David C. Cook Publishing Co., 1994.

Swindoll, Charles R. *The Strong Family*. Portland Ore.: Multnomah Press, 1991.

Warren, Ramona. *Parenting Alone, Studies for Single Parents*. Elgin, Ill.: David C. Cook Publishing Co., 1993.

Discipline

Arterburn, Stephen and Burns, Jim. *When Love Is Not Enough: Parenting through Tough Times*. Colorado Springs, Colo.: Focus on the Family Publishing, 1992.

Chase, Betty N. *Discipline Them, Love Them*. Elgin, Ill.: David C. Cook Publishing Co., 1982.

Glenn, H. Stephen; Lott, Lynn; and Nelsen, Jane. *Positive Discipline A-Z*. Rocklin, Calif.: Prima Publishing and Communications, 1993.

Nelsen, Jane. *Positive Discipline*. New York: Ballantine, 1987.

Nelsen, Jane and Lott, Lynn. *I'm On Your Side: Resolving Conflict with Your Teenage Son or Daughter*. Rocklin, Calif.: Prima Publishing and Communications, 1990.

Troubled Kids and Violence

Amstutz, Wendell and Larson, Bart. *Gangs in America*. Rochester, Minn.: National Counseling Resource Center, 1993.

Benson, Peter L. *The Troubled Journey*. Minneapolis, Minn.: Search Institute, 1993.

Cartwright, Madeline. *For the Children*. New York: Doubleday, 1993.

Dobson, James. *Love Must Be Tough*. Waco, Tex.: Word Books, 1983.

Evans, Anthony. *America's Only Hope*. Chicago: Moody Press, 1990.

Garbarino, James. *Let's Talk about Living in a World with Violence, an Activity Book for School-Age Children*. Chicago: Erikson Institute, 1993.

Kunjufu, Jawanza. *Hip-Hop vs. MAAT*. Chicago: African-American Images, 1993.

McLean, Gordon. *Danger at Your Door*. Westchester, Ill: Crossway Books, 1984.

McLean, Gordon with Jackson, Dave and Neta. *Cities of Lonesome Fear: God Among the Gangs*. Chicago: Moody Press, 1991.

Oliver, Gary Jackson and Wright, H. Norman. *When Anger Hits Home*. Chicago: Moody Press, 1992.

Cultural Issues

Bennett, William J. *The Index of Leading Cultural Indicators*. New York: Simon and Schuster, 1994.

Blythe, Dale A. with Roehlkepartain, Eugene C. *Healthy Communities, Healthy Youth*. Minneapolis, Minn.: Search Institute, 1993.

DeMoss, Robert G. *Learn to Discern*. Grand Rapids, Mich.: Zondervan Publishing House, 1992.

Dobson, James and Bauer, Gary. *Children at Risk: The Battle for the Hearts and Minds of Our Kids*. Dallas, Tex.: Word Publishing, 1990.

Family Research Council. *Free to Be Family: Helping Mothers and Fathers Meet the Needs of the Next Generation of American Children*. Washington, D.C.: Family Research Council, 1992.

Kilpatrick, William. *Why Johnny Can't Tell Right from Wrong: Moral Literacy and the Case for Character Education*. New York: Simon and Schuster, 1992.

Medved, Michael. *Hollywood vs. America: Popular Culture and the War on Traditional Values*. San Francisco: Harper Collins and Grand Rapids, Mich.: Zondervan, 1992.

Schultze, Quentin J. *Dancing in the Dark: Youth, Popular Culture, and the Electronic Media*. Grand Rapids, Mich.: W.B. Eerdmans Pub. Co., 1991.

Memories

Cut apart the following "memory ticklers" and place them in a hat or basket so each person can draw one and respond.

Describe your best friend.	What did your parents do to aggravate you?	State your biggest question about life.	Describe a typical summer day.
Recall a church memory.	What did you want to be when you grew up?	What could friends do to aggravate you?	Recall what you did on weekends.
Tell of a frightening time.	Describe an adult who made an impact on your life.	What was a major decision you had to make?	What were your dreams?
What made you laugh?	What was a common slang expression?	Name a favorite song in high school.	Describe your favorite teacher.
Tell of a silly stunt you did.	Name a favorite musical group.	Describe your favorite hangout.	In what school activity were you most involved?
What did you do to aggravate your parents?	What was your biggest worry?	What was your favorite TV program?	Describe a favorite family memory.

Violence: Yesterday and Today

For each of the categories listed in the left column below, jot down memories of violence from your youth and thoughts about violence today.

	Yesterday	Today
Television		
Movies		
Music		
Local news		
National news		
Society's reaction		
The cause (Who's to blame?)		

Kids Speak Out

For each type of violence, check all the categories that apply. If it has happened more than once, put the actual number in the appropriate box.

	It happened to me	I saw it happen to someone	It happened to someone in my family	It happened to a close friend	It happened to someone I know	I'm afraid it will happen to me
1. A fight where someone was hurt						
2. A knife fight						
3. A shooting						
4. Wounded by a bullet						
5. Killed						
6. Raped						
7. Date-raped						
8. Robbed						
9. Shaken down for money						
10. Bike or other valuable stolen						
11. Attacked by a gang of three or more						
12. Stalked on the street						
13. Received threatening notes or calls						
14. Warned to stay away from certain places						
15. A valuable possession vandalized						
16. Carried a gun to school						
17. Carried some other weapon to school						
18. Seriously considered suicide						
19. Committed suicide						
20. Observed a drug deal						

Survey Result Questions

Discuss the following questions based on the survey from last week.

- **What was the reaction of your child(ren) to answering questions about violence?**

- **What did you learn from talking with your kids that concerns you?**

- **Did you learn anything from the discussion with your child(ren) that made you feel more at ease?**

- **How did their answers differ from what you expected?**

- **Are your children's perceptions about violence different from those you hold? How does that make you feel?**

Listen to the Children

The following quotations came from grade-school-age children in Chicago who entered a writing contest called, "My Neighborhood." It was an appeal to younger residents to show civic pride. What came back shocked the adults who sponsored the contest.*

Go around the small group and take turns reading the children's reports.

Six year old: "The houses in my neighborhood look so pretty, but I don't see my neighborhood much. . . . I only go outside when I get in the car or go to school. I don't like my neighborhood because they shoot too much. They might shoot me. So, I stay in the house. . . . One time, some bullets hit our window. I was afraid. My house doesn't seem safe anymore. Maybe, I should hide under my bed. Then I won't get shot. My dog is missing. . . . Maybe they shot him. Maybe they shot him so they can rob my house. My neighborhood is getting worse. . . . Maybe, everyone should just move."

A second grader drew a large home with purple windows and a bright-faced boy in the door. But at the top of the poster board he wrote: "My neighborhood is bad . . . you will die."

Ten year old: "People get killed by shooting mostly every night."

Fifth grader: "My neighborhood is like being in jail. [I'm] scared to go outside because you were threatened that you were going to get beat up. And if you tell anybody you and the person you tell going to get shot."

Second grade girl: "One day I saw three dead bodies being pulled out of the building."

Thirteen year old: "I don't want to be one lesser black male dead. . . . My neighborhood is so bad that if you gave any fool a gun with no bullets he would try his best to shoot it. As you might know I live in a slum. Some people call it hell on earth and so do I."

Eleven year old: "These are the things in my neighborhood I see. It doesn't seem like I'm free. We cry, we weep, we can't go outside and play because our parents believe we will be killed that day."

In many of the entries the only hope expressed was in the hereafter. After giving an elaborate description of the gang killing in his neighborhood, one **third grader** wrote, "Only God can heal us."

What are these children and our children trying to teach us about growing up in a violent society? Are their concerns similar or different from your children?

---

* Jacquelyn Heard, "Young Writers' Neighborhoods Have No 'Happily Ever After,'" *Chicago Tribune*, Sect. 2, pp. 1, 2, December 14, 1992. © Copyrighted December 14, 1992, Chicago Tribune Company. All rights reserved. Used with permission.

Parents Look at Violence

Fill out the following questionnaire. Check all that apply.

1. *My definition of violence:*

2. *The evidence of violence most prevalent in our community is:*

3. *As a result of living in a more violent culture I . . .*

　　__ *am angry.*
　　__ *tolerate more.*
　　__ *feel less in control.*
　　__ *feel helpless.*
　　__ *feel like I need more help in coping.*
　　__ *feel as if my child is being impacted negatively*
　　　　by all the changes that are taking place.
　　__ *am more afraid.*
　　__ *want to move to a safer place.*
　　__ *want to equip my child to deal with*
　　　　all the struggles that are coming.
　　__ *find myself needing to be equipped.*

4. *The kinds of violence I am concerned about for my kids are . . .*

　　__ *physical assaults.*
　　__ *verbal assaults.*
　　__ *date rape.*
　　__ *shootings.*
　　__ *ordinary fighting.*
　　__ *kidnapping.*
　　__ *gang-related activities.*
　　__ *what they see on TV.*
　　__ *what they see in print.*
　　__ *what they hear on the radio.*
　　__ *what they hear in popular music.*
　　__ *random violence.*
　　__ *muggings.*

Cultural Messages

CULTURAL MESSAGE	HOW IS IT BEING SPREAD?	HOW AM I AFFECTED?	SPIRITUAL RESPONSES
1. Materialism: The most important thing in life is the ownership of possessions.			Matthew 19:21-25
2. Existentialism: Live for the moment; it's all that you have.			Hebrews 4:12, 13
3. Individualism: The most important person in your life is you.			Matthew 22:37-40
4. Hedonism: Pleasure, happiness, and fun are the primary purposes of life.			Romans 12:2
5. Secularism: God is not significant. At best He is irrelevant.			Exodus 20:1-3
6. Naturalism: Human life has no more value than an owl or a tree.			Psalm 8:3-8
7. Utopianism: Humans are basically good. Just give them a good environment, and all evil will vanish.			Romans 3:9-18
8. Anti-historicism: Truth is relative and not as important as being politically correct.			John 15:26
9. Pragmatism: If it works do it.			Psalm 119:1-4
10. Moral relativism: No absolutes. There are no rights, no wrongs.			Deuteronomy 26:16-19
11. Victimism: I am the way I am because of what other people have done to me.			Matthew 19:26

Violent Acts

How might the person(s) involved justify his or her actions based on cultural messages?

1. A group of teenage girls meet at a friend's house and try to convince her to get an abortion to eliminate her unwanted pregnancy.

2. It is Halloween. Your child is out with some friends. The group decides to start fires in abandoned buildings.

3. The Sisters, a girls' gang, attend a house party. A rival gang drives by and calls them all kinds of names. The Sisters take off after them to get revenge.

4. As the head of a major corporation, you are facing an economic slump. An opportunity presents itself to buy ad time on a television show that degrades the family. The television show is top rated and its audience profile matches the customer profile you most want to reach.

5. Your child is in a fight with a neighborhood friend. You watch and start yelling instructions to your child.

6. Your child wants to buy a video game you know is very violent. Her reason for wanting the game is that everyone else has one. You say okay because you don't want to deprive her.

7. Your neighbor hits both his spouse and children regularly. You choose to look the other way.

8. You teach your child how to get in a good lick in the middle of a football pile-up.

9. Your old boyfriend who dropped you for no apparent reason, walks down the hall with a girl you can't stand. You make plans to retaliate.

10. A family of another racial background moves into your neighborhood. You talk to your husband about selling your home and moving out of the neighborhood.

11. On a date, you get turned on physically and despite your partner's protests you force her into having sex with you.

12. You are a doctor pledged to help people live life fully. One of your older patients is terminally ill and in tremendous pain. He doesn't want to live any longer and asks you to help deliver him from the pain through an assisted suicide.

13. Your family has owned property in the inner city for years. Some might call you a slum lord. The buildings you own don't make a lot of money and would be very expensive to rehabilitate. While run down, they do provide basic shelter for people.

14. An actress has had several abortions. She pickets regularly in front of an upscale store that sells furs.

15. A movie producer wants to film a movie geared to younger audiences. The script calls for several nude scenes and dozens of acts of random violence which are designed to help box-office receipts.

16. Your mother and grandmother have quick tempers. You often lose your temper with other people and let them know exactly how you feel. When asked why, you say, "I can't help it."

17. A teenager sees a stranger with the athletic shoes he wants. He has spent his money on some other things but wants these shoes. He steals them from the stranger.

18. A group of young men decide to have a contest to see who can have sex with the most young women in a four-week time period.

19. When asked why she hurt another child, the four year old said, "They do it on television."

20. It is discovered that a known child molester was sexually abused as a child. News coverage indicates that his behavior is to be expected given his background.

What Our Kids Are Saying Today

Draw lines between the comments kids might say on the left and the corresponding cultural messages or "-isms" on the right.

KIDS' COMMENTS

1. "If my old man was rich, then I could make it."

2. "Yeah, I cheated. So what? I passed the test didn't I?"

3. "I blew it this time, but give me time. I'll get better."

4. "What's God ever done for me?"

5. "Everybody else has the latest video recorder and we've got this old one."

6. "What about me?"

7. "When you die, that's it, right?"

8. "Just because it's wrong for you, doesn't mean it's wrong for me."

9. "I'm going to enjoy myself as much as possible, now. Tomorrow may never come."

10. "Party hearty! Have a good time."

11. "All politicians lie, so what?"

CULTURAL MESSAGES

a. Materialism:
   The most important thing in life is the ownership of possessions.

b. Existentialism:
   Live for the moment; it's all that you have.

c. Individualism:
   The most important person in your life is you.

d. Hedonism:
   Pleasure, happiness, and fun are the primary purposes of life.

e. Secularism:
   God is not significant. At best He is irrelevant.

f. Naturalism:
   Human life has no more value than an owl or a tree.

h. Utopianism:
   Humans are basically good. Just give them a good environment, and all evil will vanish.

i. Anti-historicism:
   Truth is relative and not as important as being politically correct.

j. Pragmatism:
   If it works do it.

k. Moral relativism:
   No absolutes. There are no rights, no wrongs.

l. Victimism:
   I am the way I am because of what other people have done to me.

Write a comment that you think your child might make that reflects one of the above messages.

The Whole Armor of God

✔ = *That's me!*
0 = *Not me yet.*

Truth

__ The Bible is my primary source for truth.

__ I am able to discern truth from false teachings.

Righteousness

__ I am confident that I am in right standing with God because I have put my trust in Christ.

__ I may not be perfect, but holy living is my daily goal.

Peace

__ In my last crisis, I responded calmly.

__ I usually don't worry about things.

Faith

__ Although a lot of negative things have occurred to my family, I still believe God will work things out.

__ I look forward to the future.

Salvation

__ I know that Christ lives inside me.

__ The most important thing in my life is that my children become Christians.

Holy Spirit

__ I understand how to be controlled by the Holy Spirit.

__ I know how powerful the Holy Spirit is and what He can do in my life and in the lives of my children.

Bible

__ My strength and direction come from God's Word.

__ I read and explain the Bible to my children.

Prayer

__ I have established a regular devotional time.

__ I pray for my family daily.

Look at the zeros on the page. Are there holes in your armor? Your group leader has some repair suggestions.

Kids and the Media

Here are several quotes about how our culture impacts our children.

1. "Those who defend contemporary rap music, with its extravagantly brutal and obscene lyrics, do not generally condone the conduct described in the songs; they suggest, rather, that it is inappropriate to judge such material on a moral basis. By the same token, producers of movies or TV shows that seem to glorify violent or promiscuous behavior do not insist that watching these entertainments is actually good for you. Instead, they maintain that the images they create amount to a "value-neutral" experience, with no real impact on the viewer and no underlying influence on society. The apologists for the entertainment industry seldom claim that Hollywood's messages are beneficial; they argue, rather that those messages don't matter."
—Film critic Michael Medved in *Hollywood vs. America* (San Francisco: Harper Collins and Grand Rapids, Mich.: Zondervan, 1992), 23.

2. "Violence without consequence is a theme of our times. A young person told a counselor he couldn't believe he felt pain after being shot. All the shootings he had ever watched on television were of painless death or injuries."
—*Implications* magazine, Fall, 1992.

3. "The more hours of television children and adults watch, we've found the more pessimistic and deterministic they are in life—and the more they look at themselves and say, 'Since I'm not big and powerful, why bother—I have no control. Since I don't have those assets, I don't matter.' We've raised a generation of young people who, rather than being involved in meaningful things, in families, in institutions, spend more of their childhood watching the media—a media that overwhelms them, defeats them and gives them invalid role models."
—"The Second Birth Called Adolescence, a Conversation with Stephen Glenn," *Youth Worker Update*, Winter/1994, 60-61.

Continued

4. "When criticized about the content of TV shows, television executives are quick to point out that their programs merely reflect American life. Their standard retort: 'The problem is in society, not with the media.' To test the claim that TV does not mold but only mimics American life, researchers watched a week of prime-time TV . . . and concluded that any resemblance between the values and behaviors of TV characters and any actual person, living or dead, is purely coincidental."
    —*Youth Worker Update*, September 1993, 4.

5. "Violent messages in the media are aimed with particular intensity at the very young and have become a major feature of so-called children's programming."
    —Film critic Michael Medved in *Hollywood vs. America* (San Francisco: Harper Collins and Grand Rapids, Mich.: Zondervan, 1992), 247.

6. "By graduation day, the average high school student has seen 18,000 murders in 22,000 hours of television viewing. According to studies done at the Annenburg School of Communication in Philadelphia, 55 percent of prime-time characters are involved in violent confrontations once a week. . . . Dr. Leonard D. Efrom, Professor of Psychology at the University of Illinois at Chicago, conducted a 22 year study of 400 TV viewers. He concluded, 'There can no longer be any doubt that heavy exposure to televised violence is one of the causes of aggressive behavior, crime and violence in our society.' "
    —James Dobson and Gary L. Bauer, *Children at Risk* (Word Books 1990), 206, 207.

7. "According to Nielsen Media Research, teenagers ages 12-17 watch TV an average of 22 hours a week. And according to educational consultant Jawanza Kunjufu, many urban Black children watch more than twice that much. That's more hours than are spent at school and doing homework combined. We must be careful not to allow profit-driven advertisers to turn our kids into mindless junkies who will do anything for a pair of sneakers so 'I can be like Mike.' "
    —Spencer Perkins, "Confronting Today's Crisis in Youth Values," *Urban Family* magazine, Winter, 1992, 19-20.

Continued

8. "Because I know words matter, I wish my children, and kids younger than my children, would get back to innocent, hopeful lyrics. I wish their music was more about love and less graphically about intercourse. I wish their songs could be less angry and 'victimized' and more about building a better world. I wish their songs could be more like ours."
    —William Raspberry, *Washington Post*, September 18, 1993. As reported in *Youth Worker Update*, November 1993.

9. "We're raising a generation of youngsters who are numb to violence and hatred, who know death at close hand and who seriously doubt, as children never should, that they will survive to reach adulthood and middle age. Joblessness, hopelessness, miseducation, family deterioration, erosion of fundamental values—all these things contribute to our children's loss of innocence."
    —William Raspberry, *Washington Post*, July 8, 1993. As reported in *Youth Worker Update*, September 1993.

10. "In my capacity as the youth culture specialist for Focus on the Family, I and my staff transcribed [the lyrics from a] double record set and found . . .
    87 descriptions of oral sex
    117 explicit references to male and female genitalia
    226 uses of the F___ word
    163 uses of bitch when referring to women
    81 uses of the vulgarity sh__
    42 uses of ass
Among this garbage heap of lyrical imagery, the band added a reference to incest, several instances of group sex, and over a dozen illustrations of violent sexual acts. . . .
    "When it comes to the question of music's influence upon the listener, a bit of common sense is in order. We must avoid making two equally disastrous mistakes: (1) blaming all of a child's problems upon the impact of his music, and (2) dismissing any possible relationship between what a child listens to and what a child does."
    —Robert G. DeMoss, *Learn to Discern* (Grand Rapids, Mich.: Zondervan 1992), 68, 81.

Continued

11. " 'Parent's Music Resource Center's Rock Music Report' in 1985 concludes that 'the average teenager listens to rock music an average of 4 to 6 hours daily,' and that 'from grades seven through twelve the average teen listens (in six years) to 190,650 hours of music; compared to 11,000 hours listening to a teacher.' "
—*Implications* magazine, Summer 1991, Vol. 4, Issue 1, p. 2.

12. "Here's how I perceive how the electronic media has affected the kids in your youth group and set them apart from kids of twenty years ago.
- Kids in your groups are more alike. . . . They think alike, talk alike, dress alike, know the same stories, idolize the same celebrities, eat the same fast food, have the same values. . . .
- Kids in your group are more passive. . . . Thanks to the modern media, your students have learned that there is no necessary relationship between information and action.
- Kids in your group are less creative. . . . Kids who grow up with television are not used to creating their own stories, their own play, their own entertainment. They expect technology to amuse them.
- Kids in your group are busier. . . . 'Television,' writes Richard Louv in *Childhood's Future*, 'is a thief of time. . . .'
- Kids in your group are more jaded. . . . They've seen it all. Nothing shocks them. . . . Overexposure to violence, rough language, sexual situation, murder, and death has numbed kids. . . .
- Kids in your group think differently. . . . television has created a world of watchers who require fast action, quick cuts, special effects, and sound bytes to hold their attention."
—Wayne Rice, "A Word from the Editor," *Youth Worker Update*, Fall, 1991.

13. "If the beat is cool and the rapper can flow . . . sometimes you find yourself listening to stuff you don't agree with."
—"Gangsta Rap and the Culture of Violence," *Newsweek*, November 29, 1993, p. 64.

14. The Rev. Jesse Jackson has made policing rap a part of his campaign against black-on-black crime. "We're going to take the market value of these attacks on tour."
—"Gangsta Rap and the Culture of Violence," *Newsweek*, November 29, 1993, p. 64.

Hollywood vs. God's Commandments

✂ ───

God says, "You shall have no other gods before me" (Exod. 20:3), and "Worship the Lord your God, and serve him only" (Matt. 4:10).

✂ ───

God says, "You shall not make for yourself an idol" (Exod. 20:4), and "No servant can serve two masters" (Luke 16:13).

✂ ───

God says, "You shall not misuse the name of the Lord your God" (Exod. 20:7), and "Do not swear at all" (Matt. 5:34).

✂ ───

God says, "Remember the Sabbath day by keeping it holy" (Exod. 20:8).

✂ ───

God says, "Honor your father and your mother" (Exod. 20:12).

✂ ───

God says, "You shall not murder" (Exod. 20:13), and "Anyone who is angry with his brother will be subject to judgment" (Matt. 5:22).

✂ ───

God says, "You shall not commit adultery" (Exod. 20:14), and "Anyone who looks at a woman lustfully has already committed adultery with her in his heart" (Matt. 5:28).

✂ ───

God says, "You shall not steal" (Exod. 20:15).

✂ ───

God says, "You shall not give false testimony" (Exod. 20:16), and "Men will have to give account on the day of judgment for every careless word they have spoken" (Matt. 12:36).

✂ ───

God says, "You shall not covet" (Exod. 20:17), and "Be on your guard against all kinds of greed" (Luke 12:15).

✂ ───

Media Helps for Our Home

- Make all television viewing intentional. Review the television guide each week and choose the programs you will watch ahead of time.
- Watch all television programs with your child so you can turn off anything that is morally or spiritually offensive.
- For preschoolers, do not use television or a video as a baby-sitter.
- Set a maximum weekly viewing time for each child based on age. This time may not be "banked" or carried over to next week.
- Examine your own media intake. Are you digesting ungodly material and modeling inappropriate viewing or listening habits to your kids?
- Model for your kids activities such as reading and hobbies— active things that don't allow them to be passive.
- Keep a bookshelf of good Christian books and classics in the same room as the television. Read with your children often.
- Agree on family standards for video viewing. Only G or G and PG ratings, etc. Maintain "veto power" over any videos brought into the home.
- Talk with your children about things they watch and listen to. Ask questions like:
    — What are you watching (or listening to)?
    — What is this program or tape's message?
    — Is this program or video trying to persuade you to act a certain way? If so, how?
    — How does this fit with your faith?
    — Is it asking you to do anything that Jesus wouldn't approve of?

Dialog is a means of helping kids "learn to discern" which should be a goal of ours.

- Explain your reasons for your standards, and involve your older kids in the decision-making process.
- Be consistent in your standards.
- Introduce your kids to Christian and healthy secular alternatives.

A Media Plan of Action for My Family

Media issues I need to be alert for:

Media messages I'm afraid might be coming into our home:

Media messages my kids are getting that concern me:

What part of a new media policy in our home do I need to discuss with my children?

Facts and Figures About Gangs

1. Gangs have changed very little over the years. *False.* Drug involvement has drastically changed gang activity. Here are some significant dates in the development of gangs.
- 1929—The first African-American gang started. Up until this time there were school dropout-types who messed around and got into trouble, but they were unorganized.
- 1969—Before this time many strong gangs operated in cities like Chicago, Detroit, and New York, but in 1969 a group of African American's started a gang called The Crips in a high school in Los Angeles. It has since grown into one of the largest organizations in the country.
- 1980—Cocaine hit the street. Formerly, gangs were primarily social organizations, even though their activities were often "antisocial." But with the arrival of coke, a gang member could make between $300 and $600 a day. As a result, gangs became more organized, grew rapidly, and started carrying sophisticated weapons.
- Today—Gangs are involved in "gun running." Illegal sales of guns and drugs is big business.

2. African-Americans are the only race involved in gang activities. *False.* There are Hispanic, Chinese, Japanese, other Asian (Southeast Asian gangs are the most violent of all gangs) and white gangs (white supremacist or skinheads).

3. There are about one hundred thousand gang members in one city. *True.* There are 650 gangs in Los Angeles. Some seventy to one hundred thousand individuals are members of gangs in Los Angeles. In 1992 there were eight hundred gang-related killings.

4. Drive-by shootings can be related to gang initiations. *True.* But drive-by shootings can also involve several elements—turf warfare, retaliations, or the spontaneous exchange of insults (when one gang "disrespects" another).

5. The main motivation for youth who join gangs is the desire for a sense of belonging. *True.* The reason kids join a gang is to experience a kind of family, power, self-esteem, and protection—all elements of belonging. This is why many gangs are inundated with "wannabes," eight-to-ten year olds who get nothing more out of their association with the gang than a sense of belonging. Later, money may become a strong motivation. (If someone says, "You can make $300 to $600 a day," it can be hard for a young person to resist.)

6. Gangs are mainly a big city problem. In strong, small communities, gang activity is rare or nonexistent. *False.* Big cities may have the greatest numbers, but the largest growth of gang activity today is occurring in small towns and rural areas.

7. All gang members are obligated to participate in all gang activities. *False.* There are hard-core members, meaning those who have gone through initiation and are involved in gang activities twenty-four hours of the day. And there are marginal members, who drift in and out of the gang depending upon its activity. Marginal members have not made a total commitment to the gang and can be diverted from the gang.

8. Day care centers may contribute to the gang problem. *True.* As a result of their parents working, children are being placed in day care centers. There is a high rate of staff turn over in these places, and the child does not bond to one particular adult, so children often bond to peers. This pattern continues all through school, and the child learns to turn to peers not adults for support and survival.

9. Being a committed Christian can help you stay out of gang trouble. *True.* Youth who are considered religious, nerds, or straight are usually not approached by the gangs. They are considered too much of a risk.

Gang Identifiers

The following signs or attire may indicate gang involvement. HOWEVER, nongang members can and do wear some of these same things. Therefore, before you make a judgment, look for more than one sign or a combination of identifiers.

CAPS—The color of the cap or hat generally does not mean much. If the cap or hat is distinctly and consistently pointed to the left or to the right, it may be significant.

CLOTHING—Many gang members like to wear expensive Starter team jackets. Again, generally speaking the color does not mean much, but it could. Of course, these jackets are also the favorite wearing apparel of many non-gang members. Some of the Hispanic gangs favor 100 percent wool sweaters which are sometimes highly decorated.

TATTOOS—Some gang members tattoo gang symbols on their bodies. They might include such symbols as a crown and a five-pointed star, a six-pointed star, a winged heart, a spade with a "2" inside, or a Playboy bunny, top hat and cane.

HAND SIGNALS—Elaborate hand signals have been developed by many gangs. Some are as simple as always crossing the right arm over the left or vice versa. Others include very awkward-looking finger arrangements with some pointing out at odd angles and others turned in.

GRAFFITI—Many members can be seen with gang graffiti drawn on their clothing, school books, and other personal items.

JEWELRY—Some gang members wear earrings, rings, pendants bearing a five- or six-pointed star indicating their gang involvement and allegiance.

SLOGANS or CHANTS—Many gangs have their own slogans or chants.

HAIRCUTS—Some gang members have insignias shaved into their hair.

BELT BUCKLES—Often worn to the left or to the right.

BANDANNAS—Often worn on the right or left leg, or either arm or forehead.

GLOVES—Singly worn on either the right or left hand.

PANT LEG—A pant leg rolled up on the left or right side.

POCKETS—A pant pocket worn inside out.

BUTTONS—Some have buttons with their gang insignia or gang name on them.

COLORS—Some gangs, particularly Hispanic gangs, do identify with specific colors.

What Can We Do?

✂ —

Situation #1: My daughter is on cocaine and has left her children with my husband and me to care for. They seemed to be okay when they were in grade school, but now the oldest boy has already been arrested twice. He's not in school regularly, and we are afraid he is mixed up in a gang.

✂ —

Counsel to the grandparents:
- Get help and support from the church, school, police, community agency—especially someone who knows about local gangs.
- If the boy is already in a gang, it may be very difficult to get him out. Usually getting out of a gang is like getting out of the Mafia because you know too much. But it is possible. The boy could write a letter to the gang telling them that if something happens to him the police have the names of all who may be responsible.
- Leaving town usually doesn't help because they can alert other gang members in other places.
- Becoming a Christian may help. Gangs often respect a person who takes that kind of stand.
- Be firm with the children. Let them know their alternatives and consequences and stick with it.
- Try and get the child interested in other positive, structured activities.
- Try to understand the root of his rebellion and deal with that.

✂ —

Situation #2: I'm a single parent. I have to work two jobs in order to make ends meet. My daughter is thirteen, so she let's herself in the house after school. Lately she's been doing poorly in school, and I'm having to take off work to talk to the teachers. I don't like the crowd she is hanging with or the lyrics in some of the music she listens to.

✂ —

Counsel to the single parent (Adapted from "Tips for Single Parents," *Urban Family* magazine, Spring, 1994, p. 7.):
- Seriously evaluate the need to work two jobs.
- Seek help from other responsible adults in your church, neighborhood. Try to find an after-school program so your daughter is not home alone.
- Take your daughter to a correctional facility and show her what it is like to be locked up.
- Seek support for yourself.
- Be specific about your goals for yourself and your child.
- Don't be discouraged by negative statistics. Many single parents have raised fine, successful children.
- Arrange for your child to spend time with positive male adults (not alone).
- Don't be too sensitive when someone else loves and or disciplines your child.

Continued

- Don't limit your child to the things you do or don't like. Allow her to experience things with other adults.
- Be consistent with praise and discipline.
- Steer your child's friendships to families that have similar positive values.
- Don't attempt to overcompensate for the lack of a father by buying the child things or being too soft.
- Don't hold negative feelings about the child's father against the child.
- Don't be manipulated by guilt. Take charge of your household.

 —

Situation #3: My wife and I just had another baby boy. His older brother is two years old. We've heard so much about today's youth, gangs, and violence. Is there something we can start to do now to keep them from growing up and ending up in a gang?

 —

Counsel to the new parents (Adapted from Lee June, editor, *The Black Family*, Grand Rapids, Mich.: Zondervan, 1991, pp. 109, 110.):
- Pray for your children.
- Read the Bible to your children beginning at birth.
- Expose your children to written, audio, and video materials and games that help children know God.
- Encourage children to read and memorize Scripture at an early age.
- Take children to Sunday school and church.
- Clearly present the plan of salvation and encourage them to receive Christ as Savior.
- Purchase materials that accurately present Christ.
- Give them their own Bible, even before they learn to read.
- Point out Bible characters who were of your race.
- Get them involved in Christian activities.
- Teach them the biblical view of creation.
- Monitor and limit children's television viewing.
- Let them see you praying, reading the Bible, and using biblical principles in your life.
- As they face issues in school, help them view and solve the problems from a biblical perspective.
- Help to identify secular philosophies and how these often conflict with the biblical view.
- Help them to identify behaviors in themselves and their peer group that are contrary to Scripture.
- Spend time with them.
- Don't be surprised when they begin to pick out nonbiblical behavior in you. Admit you are wrong and repent.
- Teach them to tithe (give a tenth of) their earnings.
- Be good examples.

Warning Signs

Check off the at-risk behaviors that Dion exhibits.

- ❑ Becomes friends with kids you've never heard of
- ❑ Begins to exhibit a negative personality change
- ❑ Behaves in an excessively selfish manner
- ❑ Carelessly violates curfew but with "good" excuses
- ❑ Carries a weapon
- ❑ Ceases to bring friends home
- ❑ Changes dress or appearance dramatically
- ❑ Chews tobacco frequently
- ❑ Criticizes straight kids
- ❑ Defends peers' right to use drugs
- ❑ Desires to drop out of school
- ❑ Displays pictures of gang symbols in room
- ❑ Drops out of sports or extracurricular activities
- ❑ Emotionally pulls away from family
- ❑ Engages in binge drinking
- ❑ Evades questions about where he goes and what he does
- ❑ Exhibits defensiveness about friends
- ❑ Experiences deep depression
- ❑ Experiences extreme weight loss or gain
- ❑ Explodes in violent behavior or speech
- ❑ Expresses hostility toward all police
- ❑ Expresses hostility toward adults or authority figures
- ❑ Expresses seductive, promiscuous behavior
- ❑ Gets a tattoo with a gang symbol

- ❑ Gets fired from a job
- ❑ Has unusual and or secretive phone calls
- ❑ Increases isolation
- ❑ Is dissatisfied with how much freedom is allowed
- ❑ Is expelled from school
- ❑ Is involved in group fights
- ❑ Is sexually active and does not use contraceptives
- ❑ Lies and searches for loopholes
- ❑ Misses school or is tardy without your knowledge
- ❑ Often uses hand signs with friends
- ❑ Possesses drug paraphernalia
- ❑ Receives grades much lower than usual
- ❑ Refuses to use seat belts
- ❑ Resists family values
- ❑ Runs away regularly
- ❑ Smokes
- ❑ Stays out all night
- ❑ Steals things
- ❑ Talks about considering suicide
- ❑ Uses a street name
- ❑ Uses alcohol frequently
- ❑ Valuables disappear from home
- ❑ Vandalizes things
- ❑ Wears clothing of a certain style and only certain colors

The Life of Absalom

Arrange the events of Absalom's life in the correct order. If you are not familiar with this story, skim II Samuel 13:1, 8-14, 21-29, 37-39; 14:21-33; 15:1-10, 13, 14; 18:9-15, 33.

✂ —

- Absalom's sister Tamar is raped by their stepbrother Amnon, one of David's son's.

✂ —

- David heard about the rape, and he was angry, but did nothing about it.

✂ —

- Absalom said nothing to Amnon after the rape of his sister, but two years later he had Amnon killed to avenge him for raping his sister.

✂ —

- Absalom fled after killing Amnon, and went to Geshur (where his mother's father and relatives lived), and David mourned for his son every day, but did nothing.

✂ —

- David sent for Absalom to return from Gershur to Jerusalem, but David took a long time to forgive Absalom and didn't want to see him. Absalom lived in Jerusalem for two years before David allowed him to come see him.

✂ —

- After seeing David, Absalom still rebelled and got several men to follow him. He revolted against his father and ran David out of the city and made himself king.

✂ —

- David's men pursued Absalom to restore David to the throne. They found Absalom hanging from a tree. He was killed as he hung from the tree.

✂ —

- David wept bitterly and mourned the death of his son.

✂ —

Could My Child Turn Out Like Dion?

Complete a copy of this resource for each of your children. Read through the following statements and mark the strength of each asset in your child with an "X" on the scale to the right.

_____ **(Name of child)**

Has a vital, growing relationship with Jesus.

Weak _____ Strong

Has a home that is stable, secure, and loving.

Weak _____ Strong

Knows that he or she is capable.

Weak _____ Strong

Believes that he or she has unique gifts and talents to contribute.

Weak _____ Strong

Knows that he or she is not a victim, but can influence what happens to him or her.

Weak _____ Strong

Is self-disciplined and knows how to be self-controlled. He or she knows how to select from a number of possible behaviors the appropriate response in a situation.

Weak _____ Strong

Knows how to assess his or her feelings and then act appropriately.

Weak _____ Strong

Knows how to cooperate with others.

Weak _____ Strong

Is responsible.

Weak _____ Strong

Listens to others.

Weak _____ Strong

Makes judgments based upon appropriate values.

Weak _____ Strong

Based on this look at my child, here is what I feel I can do to:

Nurture areas of strength _____

_____

Strengthen areas of weakness _____

_____

The Prodigal Son Improv

Select a different dramatic or artistic style to depict your assigned scene such as: western, melodrama, mystery, slapstick comedy, musical, soap opera, docudrama, rap, etc. Add narrators, investigative reporters, camera people, directors, or anyone else to the list of suggested characters.

SCENE 1, Luke 15:11-13

Characters: Father and younger son. The older son could be present. Party goers in the far land could be added.

Situation: The youngest son of a wealthy farmer requests his share of the estate now, instead of waiting until his father dies. His father is generous, and after expressing his concern about the wisdom of the son's choice, he divides his wealth between his two sons. A few days later the younger son packs all his belongings and travels to a distant land where he spends his money freely on parties and foolish living.

SCENE 2, Luke 15:14-19

Characters: Younger son, various people in the far land, and a pig farmer.

Situation: When the son's money is gone, a great famine sweeps over the land, and he begins to starve. Finally, he persuades a local farmer to hire him to feed his pigs. The boy becomes so hungry that even the pods he feeds the swine look good to him. He finally comes to his senses and realizes that even the hired men in his father's household have plenty of food to eat. He decides to return home and confess, "Father, I have sinned against both heaven and you, and am no longer worthy of being called your son. Please take me on as a hired man."

SCENE 3, Luke 15:20-24

Characters: Younger son, father, and servants.

Situation: The boy returns home. While he is still a long distance away, his father sees him coming, and runs to welcome him. The boy begins his pitch to become a servant, but the father orders the servants to prepare a feast. The father provides for the boy the finest robe in the house, a ring for his finger, and shoes. Once the celebration begins, the father says, "This son of mine was dead and has returned to life. He was lost and is found!"

SCENE 4, Luke 15:25-32

Characters: Younger son, father, servants, and older son.

Situation: When the older son returns from working in the fields, he hears music coming from the house and asks a servant what's going on. The servant tells him that his brother is back, his father has killed the fattened calf, and a great feast is prepared to celebrate the boy's return. The older brother is angry and will not go in. When the father comes out and begs him, the older son says, "All these years I've worked hard for you and never once refused to do a single thing you told me to. In all that time you never gave me even one young goat for a feast with my friends. Yet, when this son of yours comes back after spending your money on prostitutes, you celebrate by killing the finest calf we have on the place." The father explains that he and the older son have always been together and everything that was the father's belongs to the older son, but it is right to celebrate. "Your brother was as good as dead and has come back to life! He was lost and is found!"

Looking at the Strength of Our Family

STRENGTHS OF STRONG FAMILIES	HOW MY FAMILY MEASURES UP	WORTHY IDEAS
Our family is deeply committed to each other. The family is our highest priority next to our relationship with the Lord.	I SAY ____ WEAK STRONG MY KIDS WOULD SAY ____ WEAK STRONG	
Our family is strongly committed to spending time together. We make it a point to frequently have quality time as a family unit. We frequently rearrange our schedules so we can spend time together.	I SAY ____ WEAK STRONG MY KIDS WOULD SAY ____ WEAK STRONG	
Our family practices good communication. We make an effort to listen to each other and to focus on solutions. We spend one-on-one time with each other.	I SAY ____ WEAK STRONG MY KIDS WOULD SAY ____ WEAK STRONG	
Our family shows appreciation for one another. We are able to joke and kid around at no one else's expense. We affirm each other, taking joy in each other's accomplishments.	I SAY ____ WEAK STRONG MY KIDS WOULD SAY ____ WEAK STRONG	
Our family is committed to living our life together based on scriptural principles. We know the Lord is the foundation upon which we must build our family life.	I SAY ____ WEAK STRONG MY KIDS WOULD SAY ____ WEAK STRONG	
Our family handles crises in a positive way. We see a crisis (large or small) as an opportunity to draw together instead of being drawn apart.	I SAY ____ WEAK STRONG MY KIDS WOULD SAY ____ WEAK STRONG	

The Dirty Dozen

Parenting Strategies for an Unhappy Family

1. Do your own thing whenever you want to. Don't take into account the needs of your children. No matter what it is you want to do, you owe it to yourself to do it.

2. Make sure any disagreement turns into a war. Let your children know who's boss. Prepare them for the real world.

3. Let your children know that you are always right. Anything they say should be ridiculed, criticized, and corrected according to your view of the world.

4. Give your children no say in the rules you establish. Retain the right to break, ignore, and readjust these rules at any time.

5. Consider your children as imperfect, illogical, and unrealistic. It is your perception of reality that matters, not theirs.

6. Make your kids obey your word without question or explanation.

7. Treat your career and personal interests as more important than your children. Remember, it is quality time, not the quantity of time, that counts.

8. Don't worry about praying for your kids. Don't force your spiritual views on your children by taking them to Sunday school or church. They can make their own decisions when they get older.

9. When your kids blow it, hold a grudge. Remind them often that they have made a mistake. Keep a list of all past wrongs and be prepared to throw it at them whenever you feel they deserve it.

10. Don't try to understand what your children are going through. Remind them how tough it was when you were young. Compare them to kids who do better in school, athletics, and other pursuits.

11. To keep from worrying, don't keep track of where your kids are or what they are doing. You don't want to appear noisy. Besides, what you don't know won't hurt you.

12. Let the church and school teach your children right from wrong and how to make moral decisions. Feel free to rescue your kids from bad consequences of their choices.

Clarifying the Parenting Issues

RS-9B

Answer True or False to the following statements.

1. I can do anything I please.
2. I am the boss.
3. I am always right.
4. Children have no say in setting rules.
5. My viewpoint is the only one that counts.
6. My word is final.

True False

___ ___ 1. Kids want a relationship with their parents.

___ ___ 2. Rules without relationship leads to rebellion.

___ ___ 3. Times have changed so much. Everything my kid is going through is different than what I faced.

___ ___ 4. Choose your battles wisely or you'll be battling all the time.

___ ___ 5. Kids are impressed when you say "When I was your age. . . ."

___ ___ 6. Kids will react better if they feel supported before being challenged.

___ ___ 7. Kids are under so much pressure, they don't need an environment filled with consequences.

___ ___ 8. Kids think faith is stupid.

___ ___ 9. The world is such a scary place that parents need to be especially strict with their kids.

___ ___ 10. The world is a scary place, so parents shouldn't add to it by making their kids afraid of them. Parents should avoid making any rules.

___ ___ 11. Kids are more mature these days.

___ ___ 12. This is a new day and age. Kids don't need a dad.

___ ___ 13. It's impossible for a single parent to raise a healthy child these days.

___ ___ 14. There are kids who need a "tougher" kind of love.

___ ___ 15. It's okay to rescue children from their own mistakes.

Consequences*

"Everything a parent needs to know about helping kids learn about privilege and responsibility."

EXCESSIVE CONTROL . . .

- Makes parents and teachers responsible for children's behavior.
- Prevents children from learning to make their own decisions.
- Prevents children from learning through decisions the rules for effective behavior.
- Suggests that acceptable behavior is expected only in the presence of authority figures who can enforce limits and expectations. It invites limit testing and continued negotiation of limits.
- Makes it easy for adults to be inconsistent (from guilt or fatigue).
- Creates an environment of rebellion and defiance.

NATURAL AND LOGICAL CONSEQUENCES . . .

- Hold children responsible for their own behavior.
- Allow children to make their own decisions about their actions and to experience the results.
- Teach children to experience a natural order of events.
- Teach that behavior has natural results rather than results based on the wishes of another person. It allows the child to feel powerful and secure in the outcome of events.
- Relieve adults of the frequent need to structure and restructure.
- Create less guilt and hostility in the parents resulting in a greater ability to express positive regard for the child.

PRINCIPLES FOR ESTABLISHING LOGICAL CONSEQUENCES

1. Consequences must be closely related to the positive or negative behavior.
2. Consequences must be reasonable to both adult and child.
3. Consequences should be stated in terms of privilege and responsibilities.
4. Consequences should be established prior to the event by mutual agreement of both child and adult.
5. Consequences should be established in an environment of unqualified love and mutual respect.
6. Consequences, once established, should have consistent follow-through.
7. Consequences should be enforced with dignity and respect.
8. When something unanticipated occurs, handle it as close to a natural consequence as possible, avoiding overkill and punitive responses. Then, if it's likely to be a problem in the future, agree on different consequences.
9. Family meetings provide excellent opportunities for children to be involved in decisions regarding consequences.

* Adapted from Stephen Glenn, Participant's Workbook, *Developing Capable People Manual* (Provo, Utah: Sunrise, Inc., 1991), pp. 7.14, 7.17. Used with permission.

What I Want to Build into My Child

Pretend it is your ninetieth birthday. You still are quite active. You walk into your home after your morning round of tennis and "Surprise!" Your children and close friends have thrown you a birthday party. During the course of the party your children get up to talk about the impact your life has had on theirs. What would you want them to say?

I. Write a six-sentence speech you'd like one of your children to give about you.

II. If these are the things I want my children to say about me, I need to be building these qualities into their lives now.

1. What personality characteristics would I like them to be noted for?

2. What perceptions about themselves do I want them to hold?

3. What core values and beliefs would I like them to cherish?

4. What skills do I think my children will need?

5. How do I plan on teaching them?

Parenting Strategies

✂ —

1. You try to nurture an internal control in your child so that he or she is not dependent on adults to make wise decisions.

✂ —

2. You are teaching your child about life by modeling good decision making in the way you communicate.

✂ —

3. You have a long-term relationship with your child. It's obvious there is a pattern of good communication.

✂ —

4. Your child is encouraged to assess the situation and respond to what he or she sees taking place. You ask your child to think about other possible behaviors than the chosen one.

✂ —

5. You work to create an environment of love in your home. If necessary, you are willing to use a "tough love" kind of approach to get your child's attention.

✂ —

6. Your child is encouraged to learn from what has happened.

✂ —

7. You work hard at trying to develop a firm, yet, relationally consistent environment. You consistently model good communication.

✂ —

8. You try to stay calm no matter what "button is pushed." There is no yelling, screaming, intimidating, manipulating, crying, or gnashing of teeth. You don't try to teach when your feelings are too intense.

✂ —

9. You ask for your child's side of the story. You don't assume anything. Even though another adult has told his or her version of the story, you explore your child's perceptions of what happened.

✂ —

10. You listen. You seek to understand both content and feelings.

✂ —

11. You anticipate challenges and talk to your child about them ahead of time.

✂ —

12. You pray regularly for your child. You aren't afraid to call on the Lord in times of trouble.

✂ —

13. You don't tell your child how to respond. You explore with your child what has happened, why it happened, the consequences, and how a negative situation might be avoided in the future. The child learns through the interaction while you show respect for the other adults involved in the child's life.

✂ —

Continued

✂ — ✂ — — — — — — — — — — — — — — — —

14. Your child is able to identify feelings, pinpoint what triggered them, and then analyze what and why certain things were happening.

✂ — ✂ — — — — — — — — — — — — — — — —

15. It's obvious that you as the parent have an "goal" in mind for your child, a plan for what you want to build into his or her life. You know how to work that plan.

✂ — ✂ — — — — — — — — — — — — — — — —

16. You are willing to bring in other persons to help. You don't try to make your child feel any worse than he or she actually feels.

✂ — ✂ — — — — — — — — — — — — — — — —

17. You have established a consequential environment in the home. As much as possible, the consequences flow naturally from the child's actions.

✂ — ✂ — — — — — — — — — — — — — — — —

18. Your interaction focuses in on your child and his or her actions, not the behavior of others. Your child cannot control what other people do.

✂ — ✂ — — — — — — — — — — — — — — — —

19. The principles in your home are based on spiritual roots and values.

✂ — ✂ — — — — — — — — — — — — — — — —

20. You don't let your child off the hook nor do you allow the hook to be set too deeply.

✂ — ✂ — — — — — — — — — — — — — — — —

21. As a parent, you aren't overly permissive. Thus, your child isn't able to explain his or her actions away by blaming others. You don't rescue your child from the consequences.

✂ — ✂ — — — — — — — — — — — — — — — —

22. You aren't overly strict. You are balanced in your approach to your child. Your child will pay the consequences, but he or she won't be thrown into a "locked cell."

✂ — ✂ — — — — — — — — — — — — — — — —

Setting: Randy's room

Parent *(entering room)*: Randy, do you have a minute? I need to talk with you.

Randy *(seated on bed with earphones on)*: Not right now. I'm busy.

Parent: Randy, I really need to talk with you now *(sits on bed)*.

Randy: All right, what do you want?

Parent: Randy, I received a call from your principal this afternoon. Do you have any idea what it might be about?

Randy: Yeah . . . it was the fight at lunchtime, wasn't it? But it wasn't my fault. It just happened.

Parent: I heard what the principal, Mrs. Mitchell, had to say. Now I want to hear about it from your perspective.

Randy: Mrs. Mitchell must really hate me.

Parent: No, she's disappointed in the way you responded to the situation. But she doesn't hate you. Now, tell me what happened.

Randy: Well, I was eating lunch with my friends when those guys you think are gangbangers came by the table and started messin' with us. I know we've talked about how to act around guys like that, but I just kinda lost it.

Parent: Messin' with you?

Randy: Yeah, you know. They started grabbing our food and throwin' it around.

Parent: Go on.

Randy: Then, they grabbed my homework—the stuff I worked on all weekend—and threw it around the room. I was so angry.

Parent: So, when you got angry what went through your head?

Randy: I remembered what you taught me about not losing my temper when I get angry. I tried to think of some better ways of dealing with it. But . . . I got so mad that I grabbed Tony and punched him.

Parent: What happened then?

Randy: When he fell down, I jumped on him. I was going to hit him again, but a security guard ran over and pulled me off.

Parent: After that . . . ?

Randy: I don't know exactly. The guard took me to the principal's office. I heard some of

the other guys got into a big fight after that. It was pretty awful. What did Mrs. Mitchell say?

Parent: Your story is in line with what was reported to her. How are you feeling now?

Randy: Not real good. My hand hurts . . . that boy's got a hard head! And I've got the feeling I'm in trouble. Tony and those guys will be out to get me now. I'm afraid of what they might do to me.

Parent: Randy, this isn't the first time this year this has happened.

Randy: I know. I'm trying! But it's so hard.

Parent: Randy, I'm disappointed that you chose the response you did. What could you have done differently?

Randy: I dunno. They were being real jerks. It would have been impossible to ignore them. But . . . I guess I could have gone over to one of the security people and asked for help or just gotten up and left.

Parent: Why didn't you do that?

Randy: Well, I didn't want to look like I was some kind of weakling! Telling an adult is like admitting I can't handle things. It was just real confusing. Everything happened so fast.

Parent: Well, I can understand the confusion, especially in the midst of a situation like that. But, Randy, if those boys were gangbangers, who knows what could have happened! Haven't we talked about how to get out of situations like that? There had to be a better way of dealing with it.

Randy: I know. But talking about it at home is different than when you're dealing with it right then in school. It was really hard. Man, if those guys weren't such jerks I wouldn't be in such trouble!

Continued

Parent: I agree, they acted like jerks. But you know what we've always said "The only—"

Randy: I know, I know. "The only person you can control in a relationship is you."

Parent: Well, think about it a bit more. Because you know you're going to be faced with situations like that in the future at your school. You've got to choose better. Now, what do you think are the consequences of all this?

Randy: Besides having a sore hand and being afraid to see those guys again? Well, Mrs. Mitchell told me I'm suspended for a week.

Parent: That's right. You will be held responsible, though, for all your school work for every day during the suspension.

Randy: Oh, man.

Parent: It also means you won't be eligible to play basketball during the suspension.

Randy: What? That's not fair! The league playoffs are next week. I can't miss the playoffs. The team needs me.

Parent: Did coach lay out the rules for participation early in the year?

Randy: Well, yeah . . .

Parent: I know you weren't even thinking about it, but you did understand the rules?

Randy: Yes, but I . . . this is bogus!

Parent: Randy, you knew the rules. You knew what the consequences were. By choosing to fight . . . you pay the consequences.

Randy: But it's not fair.

Parent: It might not seem fair to you but who made the choice to fight? *(Silence for a few moments.)* Randy, whose choice was it?

Randy: Well . . . mine. But I wasn't thinking.

Parent: I know. It's really hard. But do you remember what I've taught you about making decisions?

Randy: Yeah . . . that it's best to do what Jesus would do.

Parent: That's right. What would Jesus want you to do to clean up this situation?

Randy: Oh, come on! I don't want to apologize to Tony.

Parent: I know you don't, Son, but it seems to me that if you're old enough to behave yourself into a situation, you're big enough to try to make it right again.

Randy: All right. I'll apologize.

Parent: When?

Randy: I'll call tonight.

Parent: How are you feeling right now?

Randy: I don't know. I guess I feel angry at myself because I chose what I knew was wrong. And I'm real sad because I'm going to miss some big games and I'm worried that people are going to be mad at me for a while. I'm mad at Tony and those guys he hangs out with for being jerks and putting me in this situation in the first place.

Parent: This has happened before, Randy. What do you think you can do to make sure it doesn't happen again?

Randy: I don't know.

Parent: I want you think about it some more. You do seem to do some irrational things when you get angry. You need to think it through a bit more. We're not done talking about all of this. I love you but I want you to know that I am disappointed in your decisions today.

Randy: Is that all?

Parent: No, there's one more thing. Do you remember what happened to your brother?

Randy: He got in big trouble. You had to call the police on him.

Parent: Do you know why?

Randy: I guess 'cause he never wanted to follow the rules. He was a real jerk about everything.

Parent: That's right. Randy. That was the toughest thing I've ever done. He just wouldn't work with us here. We finally had to force him to accept some pretty major consequences. Randy, I'll be as tough on you as you need. But I don't want to be all that tough. If you need someone else to talk to, I'd be glad to call Mike at the church and see if he would spend some time with you.

Randy: No, that's okay.

Parent: Okay, then. Would you mind if we prayed about this situation now? I want to make sure we get God's help on all this.

A Firm Foundation

Character Quality	Reasons It Is Needed	Biblical Basis
1. A commitment and love for Jesus Christ, our Lord and Savior.		
2. An understanding of the benefits believers have in Jesus Christ.		
3. A knowledge and understanding of ethnic history, starting with the Bible.		
4. A strong work ethic.		
5. An understanding and desire for the God-instituted family.		
6. Respect for authority.		
7. An appreciation for knowledge, education, and wisdom.		
8. Self-dignity, self-control, and self-respect.		
9. A respect for others.		
10. A basic understanding of financial systems.		

Character Quality Checklist and Goals

Put a check (✔) before the areas you personally need to improve. Put a "c" by it if it is something you need to work with your child on.

Me   My child

___   ___   My children see me reading the Bible. It has motivated them to read the Bible, too.

___   ___   When we encounter a crisis in our family, my children see me trusting God. By watching my example, they learn to pray and turn to God's Word for comfort and wisdom.

___   ___   We have several ethnic history books in our home. The children use them.

___   ___   We talk often about our historical roots.

___   ___   I demonstrate hard work, inside and outside the home. The children know the benefit of hard work.

___   ___   We have struggles, but I believe our family is important and worth fighting for.

___   ___   My children want to get married and have a family.

___   ___   My children have witnessed me handling authority figures firmly but with respect.

___   ___   I still take a class from time to time to improve myself.

___   ___   My children want to learn a trade or go to college.

___   ___   In our home we don't allow any kind of put-downs about ourselves, other people, or any race.

___   ___   As a family, we have projects we do together to help other people.

___   ___   We have a financial plan for our family.

___   ___   I'm teaching my children about finances.

In what areas do I need help in?

In what areas do I need to help my child?

What do I plan to implement this week?

The Church and the Development of Youth

As the oldest and most influential institution controlled by the black community, the black church has a crucial educational and spiritual role to play in the development of African-American youth. The following recommendations can be made to ensure the continued positive impact of the black church on our young people. *

1 It is important that black children feel good about themselves in order to develop positive self-concepts. Churches can provide Sunday school, Bible school, and a variety of Christian reading materials that portray black people and black family life in accurate and positive images.

2 Gainful employment provides financial independence as well as self-esteem. The church can employ African-Americans in areas of maintenance, tutoring, nursery school attendants, and other meaningful services. This also teaches job responsibilities and employment socialization.

3 Youth need adults who are willing to spend quality time listening to their concerns and providing relevant guidance. The church can develop and implement mentoring programs to match youth with positive role models and Christian adult companions.

4 It is often necessary to supplement the efforts of public education to ensure that black children receive an adequate foundation for higher education and training. The church can develop and maintain tutoring programs that assist young people to achieve early academic success.

5 Quality child care is one of the most expensive items in a family's budget. The church can provide low-cost child care at the church facility for working parents.

6 The talents and affiliations of black church members are often underutilized. The black church should use all of its resources to ensure appropriate knowledge and receipt of public, tax-funded services. Develop a network of church members with professional and personal ties to organizations or agencies that are charged with providing services for children. Those members can serve as effective advocates for people most in need.

7 The black church cannot afford to be passive when it comes to the education of its children. It can require accountability of elected officials on state and local school boards. Also, churches should urge active parental involvement in Parent-Teacher Associations.

8 Black youth need relevant and straightforward information and guidance, especially from a Christian perspective. Churches should provide seminars and forums on topics of interest to the Christian adolescent; topics could include substance abuse, sexuality, career planning, male-female relationships, relationships with parents, relationships with non-Christian peers, political awareness, and spiritual struggles.

* Adapted from Bonita Pope Curry, *The Black Family* (Grand Rapids, Mich.: Zondervan, 1991), pp. 120, 121.

Keeping Kids Out of Trouble

Make sure your children understand the consequences of unlawful behavior or befriending other youths who disrespect the law.

1. "If young toughs tell you, 'Come and join us'—turn your back on them! 'We'll hide and rob and kill,' they say. 'Good or bad, we'll treat them all alike. And the loot we'll get! All kinds of stuff! Come on, throw in your lot with us; we'll split with you in equal shares.' Don't do it, son! Stay far from men like that, for crime is their way of life, and murder is their specialty. When a bird sees a trap being set, it stays away, but not these men; they trap themselves! They lay a booby trap for their own lives. Such is the fate of all who live by violence and murder. They will die a violent death" (Prov. 1:10-19, TLB).

2. Many states have what is commonly called an "accountability law" making everyone in the company of someone who commits a crime equally guilty. Review it carefully with your young person. Where that law exists, proving you "didn't do anything wrong" won't help at all. The only hope is to stay away from where anything "is going down."

3. Make an appointment for your family to talk with someone in the police or juvenile justice department. Have that person give your family a tour of a juvenile detention center, prison, or jail. Help your children understand the consequences of petty crimes and serious offenses. Also, discuss the long-range results of having a criminal record after a jail or prison sentence.

4. Make sure your children respect your city's curfew. The lives of many young people could have been saved if their parents would have insisted that they obey that one rule.

5. Teach your children to respect authority. This should start in the home, at an early age. First, they should respect you as the parent. Then they should respect other adults.

6. Your children should learn this respect from you as they watch you interact with those in authority over you. There is a way to be firm, yet stay in control and treat others with consideration.

Continued

7. Tell your children to be respectful toward the police. They should not call the police names, or accuse them of misconduct. Remember, the police have the authority, the law, and a gun on their side.

8. Teach your children how to handle harassment and avoid brutality. Make sure your children know that they do not have to give out any information. If the police approaches them, they can give their name and address, but they do not have to answer any other questions. Instruct your children to ask, "Am I under arrest? For what reason am I being arrested? I prefer to remain silent until I contact my parents or my attorney." Gordon McLean, the director of the juvenile justice ministry of Metro Chicago Youth for Christ issues a card to the young people he serves that says:

> "If you are arrested, do not resist or get smart with officers. You have a right to remain silent. Don't discuss your case with the police or State's Attorneys at the station. You have a right to a lawyer of your own. Insist on talking to your lawyer or a public defender. Keep this card on you. Call your attorney before you say anything to an arresting officer."

9. Get to know an attorney before a crisis occurs. Select someone you know and trust. Have his or her number handy and have him or her meet you at the station.

10. Provide your young person with the name and phone number of the trusted lawyer.

11. If your child is harmed, do your best to take pictures of your child before he or she is cleaned up. Get medical attention, and get a copy of the medical report. File a complaint and continue to call and ask about the status of your complaint.

12. Have a law enforcement officer talk to your church youth group or block club about these matters. Be informed!

When Your Child Has Witnessed Violence

If your child has witnessed a violent crime or someone close to him or her dies as a result of a violent act, here are some suggestions for helping your child cope.

- Hug your child.

- Allow your child to talk openly and freely about what happened. If you don't feel comfortable listening, have your child talk to someone else (minister, counselor at school, crisis counselor, etc.). It is very important to allow the child to talk it out. This is not the time to say, "I don't want to hear it any more."

- If your child is having a hard time with fear, he or she may need additional support temporarily. You may need to transport your child to and from school for a while.

- Identify adults that will be able to help if you are not available. Help your child feel confident that someone will be there for your child, if he or she wants to talk or is feeling the need for help.

- Reassure your child that it is okay to feel scared, sick to the stomach, upset, or mad about what has happened. Allow your child to cry. Cry with your child. This is not a time to hold back emotions. This needs to be communicated especially to older boys who may think they have to act tough. Encourage your child to express his or her feelings.

- Watch for changes in your child's patterns. If he or she is unusually quiet, has trouble eating, is afraid to go outside, etc., these may be indications that your child needs counseling or further help dealing with feelings.

- Nighttime may be difficult for a while. Your child may need to sleep with the light on. You may have to spend extra time with your child before he or she is able to fall asleep.

"Deliver Us from Evil"

RS-13C

Read aloud the bold-faced lines. Your leader will respond with the lines in normal print.

Love must be sincere.

And I call you to love even those you hate. How many violent people have never felt a sincere love?

Hate what is evil.

There is so much evil we just accept and do nothing about.

Be devoted to one another in brotherly love.

There is power in the unity of Christian love.

Honor one another above yourselves.

We have to be there for one another. It's too difficult to be alone.

Never be lacking in zeal, but keep your spiritual fervor.

How can we go to battle against violence with a wishy-washy faith?

Be joyful in hope.

Jesus said that He would never leave or forsake us. With Him by our side we needn't lack hope.

Be patient in affliction.

All things work towards the good for those who love the Lord even when we don't understand God's timing.

Be faithful in prayer.

It is your greatest weapon as a parent.

Share with God's people who are in need.

Look around this room. Someone is hurting. An old African proverb says, "It takes a whole village to raise a child." It takes a whole church to raise a child these days.

Practice hospitality.

Your home could be the warmth that another family needs.

Bless those who persecute you.

Trying to counteract a violent world will make you enemies. Will you be willing to bless them in the midst of your frustration with them?

Bless and do not curse.

Cursing is a violent act that requires no courage.

Rejoice with those who rejoice.

May their joy be yours.

Mourn with those who mourn.

In a violent world, you will need to learn this. Is the church the place where mourners find comfort?

Continued

"Deliver Us from Evil" (continued)

RS-13C

...in harmony ... ... revenge.

...en the body is ... ...ecomes so vicious.
difference for the s...

Do not be proud.

...to avenge, I will repay," says

Pride gets in the w... ...s. There is a judgment. There is
talents to serve ou...

Be willing to ass... ...emy is hungry, feed him or
low position.

Those who have b... ...e food you give will give the
required to give m... ...ength to start a different kind of
the answer to ano...

Do not be conce... ...e is thirsty, give that person
...g to drink.

There is enough i... ...ange a life.
humble you.

Do not repay any... ...overcome by evil.

Violence begets v... ...d over all. He is King. Keep your
...sed on Him.

Be careful to do what is right in the eyes of God.

Overcome evil with good.

We are called to live holy and blameless lives.

Go, make disciples . . . loving those you encounter in the name of the Lord . . . make a difference in the life of your healthy child, in your community. . . . You can raise kids in a violent culture. . . . If you don't, who will?

Live at peace with everyone.

Blessed are the peacemakers.